THE
PUBLIC SPEAKER'S
JOKE BOOK

THE PUBLIC SPEAKER'S JOKE BOOK

by

Kevin Goldstein-Jackson

PAPERFRONTS
ELLIOT RIGHT WAY BOOKS
KINGSWOOD, SURREY, U.K.

Typeset in 10/12pt Times by County Typesetters, Margate, Kent.

Made and Printed in Great Britain by Cox & Wyman Ltd., Reading, Berkshire.

Contents

Dedication

This book is dedicated to my two young daughters, Sing Yu (who kindly helped sort the jokes into alphabetical order) and Kimberley.

The Public Speaker's Joke Book is also dedicated to all my friends and acquaintances who kindly made suggestions for it; and to my wife, Mei Leng, in the hope that she will prefer this book to my cheque book!

Introduction

My last joke book had astronomical sales (three astronomers bought a copy of it) so the publishers asked me to write THE PUBLIC SPEAKER'S JOKE BOOK.

This book contains 561 jokes, which have been listed alphabetically under various subject headings, although sometimes it has been very difficult to decide under which of a number of equally appropriate headings a joke should appear.

There is also a Directory section to assist in finding the most appropriate joke for the occasion.

The term 'public speaker' has been used in its widest sense: anyone who at any time has to speak in public – not only people speaking at parties, dinners, receptions, conventions – but even the much more difficult task of filling in time at a children's party when the magician has got lost and will be arriving late (just let the children laugh and groan by using some of the jokes in the Questions section and other suitable jokes in this book).

The jokes range from the old to the new, from the bold to the slightly blue, and from groan-making to side-splitting.

In the interests of equality there are sections of jokes about Boyfriends and Husbands.

Hopefully, there is something in this book suitable for every public speaker. But try to choose the right joke for the right audience. A sick joke should not be brought up in polite conversation.

Some of the jokes mention certain towns (like Basingstoke and Bournemouth) but most of these can easily be changed to the place where the public speaker is speaking or to a similarly appropriate town or city.

If you are nervous about making a speech, start with a modest apology – like: 'Before I begin my speech I'd like to warn you that I will be talking while suffering from a severe handicap – I'm sober.'

Remember that a bore is a person with nothing to say who insists on saying it. A good speech is a bit like a beautiful woman's skirt – short enough to attract great interest, but long enough to cover the essentials.

If a joke 'falls flat' just ignore the reaction and continue, or say something like: 'Well, now I know why that joke cost less than a penny.' (Which it did – just divide the number of jokes in this book by its modest purchase price.)

If anyone should heckle, simply comment: 'Thank you for giving us a piece of your mind. It's a pity you don't have much left.' Or you could say: 'I hear you are going into hospital next week for a brain operation – the doctors hope to give you one.' Or 'The last time I saw something that looked like you I threw it a peanut.'

Finally, you may like to know that a psychologist has proved that jokes are healthy because laughter helps people to relax, and laughter and fun 'give your heart, lungs, face, shoulders and diaphragm a really good workout.'

I sincerely hope that some of the jokes in this book will help you to spread some health and happiness to your next audience.

Good luck – and best wishes.

KG-J

Directory to the Book

On this, and the following eight pages is the Directory to the 561 jokes in this book.

If you are *not* searching for a particular joke/subject and are just reading this book for fun (or there's nothing else to read in the toilet) then just skip all these pages and start on page 21.

The numbers given below refer to the number of the joke and *not* to the page number.

Work: *Joke no.* 319, 557
Writers: *Joke no.* 291

Yugoslavia: *Joke no.* 558

Zoos: *Joke no.* 559, 560, 561

JOKES

A

ACCOUNTANT

1. The company personnel department had carefully interviewed thirty-eight people for the job of assistant to the financial director.

The chief executive thought that one candidate – Charles – seemed ideal. Charles had been to a major public school. Not only was he a qualified accountant, but Charles also had a masters degree in business administration. He seemed fully aware of the latest creative accountancy techniques.

'Charles,' said the chief executive, 'we've decided to offer you the job. And as you're so well qualified we've decided to start you off on a slightly higher salary than the one advertised. We'll pay you £36,000 a year.'

'Thank you,' replied Charles. 'But how much is that per month?'

ACTORS

2. The young actress was delighted to get a part with real meat in it. She had to dress up as a bun for a commercial for hamburgers.

3. I was once asked to play the part of a vampire's victim in a Hollywood movie, but I turned it down. I don't do bit parts.

4. The leading actress was most upset on her opening night. She only received seventeen bouquets of flowers. Yet she had paid the florist to send twenty.

5. Middle-aged American actresses all seem to go to the same breed of horse to get their teeth.

AFFAIRS

6. A friend of mine has just spent ten thousand pounds on a little peace and quiet. His little piece wanted the ten thousand to keep it quiet from his wife.

7. The husband was furious. 'Is it true you've been having an affair with John?' he angrily asked his wife.

'Yes,' replied the wife.

'Then,' said the husband, 'I'm going round to his house and I'll teach him a lesson . . .'

'But darling,' said the wife, 'couldn't you take a few lessons from him instead and then I wouldn't need to have to have an affair?'

AGE

8. I wouldn't say my wife tells lies about her age – but does she really expect people to believe that she gave birth to our son at the age of three?

9. You know you're old when you recall that in your youth a kiss happened at the end of a beautiful evening. Today, a kiss means it's the start of a *fantastic* evening.

10. I think I've just reached the out-age. When you reach fifty everything seems to spread out, fall out or wear out!

ANTIQUES
11. I once went into an antiques shop and picked up an old-fashioned telephone.

'That's very rare, sir,' said the shop assistant. 'It was used by the ancient Britons.'

'But surely,' I said, 'the telephone hadn't been invented then.'

'That,' replied the shop assistant, 'is what makes that particular telephone so rare.'

12. I know a man who makes a very good living by buying junk and selling antiques.

BANKS
13. 'Why,' asked Mr. White, 'are you still overdrawn at the bank?'

'I don't know,' replied his wife. 'They sent me a bank statement last month and a letter saying I was five hundred pounds overdrawn. Then they sent me another letter insisting I pay the five hundred pounds within seven days. So I paid it promptly. I immediately wrote them a cheque for the money.'

BARGAIN
14. A bargain is something you buy that is cheaper than something you really want or need.

BAT

15. The bat was very tired. It sunk lower and lower until it did not have enough energy to flap its wings any more and so it flopped to the ground.

After a few minutes it crawled along the grass until it came to the old trees where it lived. Then it suddenly raced towards the trees, stopped when it almost hit them, then went backwards. Then it raced towards the trees again.

It did this so many times that I became curious.

'Why are you racing towards the trees, stopping, going backwards, then racing towards them again?' I asked.

The bat sighed, then said (for it was a talking bat): 'I was very run down and so I need to charge my bat-trees!'

16. What bat is good at knowing all the letters?
An alpha-bat.

BEES

17. Why were there so many bees in the toilet at the petrol station?
Because they saw the sign advertising BP.

BIRTH

18. The new doctor was making his round of the maternity ward and the first five women he saw were all expecting their babies on the same day: 28th March.

The doctor moved on to look at the sixth patient.

'And when is your baby expected?' asked the doctor.

'I don't know,' replied the woman, 'I didn't go to the office party like the other women in here did.'

19. When my husband was born it wasn't a stork that delivered him – it was a vulture.

20. When Claude's wife was expecting their second child he told his three-year-old son that soon a giant stork would be arriving and it would land on the chimney of their house. In the stork's beak would be a wonderful present.'

'Oh,' said Claude's son, 'I hope it will be quiet and won't upset mummy. A giant bird suddenly arriving like that might give her a shock. And that wouldn't be any good as you know you made her pregnant and she's expecting a baby.'

BIRTHDAYS
21. When I was a child my family were so poor that the only thing I got on my birthday was a year older.

22. My husband said he wanted a tie for his birthday that matched the colour of his eyes – but where can you find a bloodshot tie?

23. My wife refuses to use Inter Flora for people's birthdays. She says she doesn't think people would like margarine as a present.

24. It's my wife's birthday tomorrow. Last week I asked her what she wanted as a present.

'Oh, I don't know,' she said. 'Just give me something with diamonds.'

That's why I'm giving her a pack of playing cards.

BOOKS

25. *Great Eggspectations* by Charles Chickens.

26. *Big Celebrations* by Annie Versary.

27. *How Sherlock Holmes Quickly Solved Crimes* by L.M.N. Tree.

28. *In The Soup* by Minnie Stroney.

29. What do you get if you throw a copy of *The Canterbury Tales* in the air?
A flying Chaucer.

30. What was enormous, very heavy, lived a long time ago and liked *Wuthering Heights* and *Jane Eyre*?
A Bronte-saurus.

31. My next book is about two families who constantly fight and argue – it's a work of friction!

32. My books of prose may be bad, but they could be verse.

33. I once knew an author who changed his name to biro because he wanted a pen name.

BORES

34. A bore is someone who opens his mouth and puts his own feats in it.

BOYFRIENDS

35. My boyfriend is a kung-fu expert. Last night he hit an insect on his side and broke one of his own ribs.

36. On my first date with my boyfriend I asked him if I could hold his hand, and he said: 'I can manage, thank you. It isn't very heavy.'

BUILDERS

37. I once knew a builder who smiled every time he had a house maid.

38. Three Irishmen were hired to work on a building site and were asked to sign a contract before they started work.

The first Irishman signed his contract with a cross because he couldn't write his name, and the second Irishman signed with two crosses.

'Why the two crosses?' asked the builder.

'Because I've got a double-barrelled name,' came the reply.

The third Irishman signed the contract with three crosses and said: 'I have a double-barrelled name, and the third cross is my degree in brickwork from the polytechnic.'

BUS TRAVEL

39. The first time I went to Bournemouth I wanted to visit Compton Acres Gardens in Poole. I joined a bus queue, and as a bus approached I asked the elderly lady in front of me: 'Excuse me, does this bus go to Compton Acres?'

'Yes,' replied the lady, 'just get off the bus two stops before the stop I get off.'

BUSINESS PEOPLE

40. The tired, exhausted businessman had felt compelled to drink more than he could really cope with at a business lunch at which he had lost his firm's major client.

The businessman staggered back to the office and asked his gorgeous secretary: 'Can you give me something to ease my pain?'

'How about something tall and cold?' replied the secretary.

'Don't!' said the businessman. 'Don't bring my wife into it.'

41. When I asked my boss for a salary rise because I was doing the work of three men he said he couldn't increase my pay, but if I told him the names of the three men he'd fire them.

42. I'm always delighted when people stick their noses in my business – my company makes paper tissues.

43. My husband's business is rather up-and-down – he makes yo-yos.

44. When Bernard got fired from his last job they were really tough. They made him hand back his keys to the executive toilets, return his company credit card, give back his company car, and even give back his ulcer!

45. Last night I discovered why my boss hired *me* rather than all the other candidates to be his deputy. Over a lengthy business dinner he admitted that when he interviewed all the other candidates they seemed to be the cleverest, most dynamic people in the world.

Yet when he interviewed me, I managed to convince him that *he* was the cleverest, most dynamic person in the world.

46. Another friend of mine is a very successful businessman. He started with five thousand pounds – now he owes fifty-five million.

47. I once knew a man who was always travelling abroad for business meetings. One trip lasted two whole months and towards the end of it he could stand it no longer and went to the local brothel.

'I would like your most bored, tired, fat lady,' he said.

'Why do you want someone like that?' asked the surprised madam.

'Because,' replied the businessman, 'I've been away for so long I'm homesick for my wife!'

48. I once knew a couple who were in the iron and steel business – she did the ironing, while he went out stealing.

BUTTERFLY
49. Why couldn't the butterfly go to the dance?
Because it was a moth ball.

C

CABARET
50. A friend of mine once went to a naughty cabaret show where the stripper was so ugly that when she was half-way through her act the audience shouted: 'Put them on! Put them on!'

CAROL SINGING
51. When I was younger I used to love Carol singing. Now I'm older I love Carol sighing.

CARS
52. I bought a car that was rust free. The car dealer sold me the car for two thousand pounds and didn't charge anything for all the rust.

53. A friend of mind has a car that is so old it's insured against fire, theft and Viking raids.

54. I was nearly late arriving at this meeting. The journey from my home was extremely arduous and I had to walk the last few miles after I suddenly lost control of my car – the finance company re-possessed it.

55. The car dealer tried to sell me a car that he said was in mint condition. It had a hole in the middle.

56. I know a man whose car is in such bad condition that when he took it to the garage and told a mechanic: 'Give it a service' – they gave it a burial service.

57. Frederick: 'My cousin thinks he's a car.'

Julia: 'What does he do?'

Frederick: 'He makes car-like noises and jogs along the road instead of the pavement. When he gets to a petrol station he pours petrol in the back pocket of his trousers.'

Julia: 'Shouldn't you do something about it?'

Frederick: 'I suppose I should, but I need the money he gives me. Every Saturday he pays me £35 to give him a good wax and polish.'

58. What is the difference between an ancient car and a class in school?

Not much – they both have lots of nuts and a crank at the front.

59. When buying an old second-hand car always insist on getting one with heated rear windows. That way, in winter you can warm your hands while you're pushing it.

CATS

60. Outraged customer: 'This cat you sold me is absolutely useless!'

Petshop owner: 'What's wrong with it? It looks perfectly all right to me.'

Outraged customer: 'When you sold it to me you promised it would be a good cat for mice. Yet every time it sees a mouse it runs away and hides.'

Petshop owner: 'Well, isn't that a good cat for mice?'

CHILDREN

61. This morning my son asked me if I could tell him what makes the sky blue. I told him to look it up in an encyclopaedia.

At lunchtime he asked me how long it would take to boil an ostrich egg. I said I didn't know.

This afternoon my son asked me how far away from Earth is the planet Pluto. I said I didn't know.

Earlier this evening he asked me how deep a fathom is in metres. I said I didn't know, but he could look it up in a dictionary.

Just before I left to come to this meeting my son asked me: 'Who was the first King of England?' I said I couldn't remember.

Then he asked: 'Do you mind me asking you so many questions?'

I told him: 'Of course not.' How else will he learn things if he doesn't ask questions?

62. My youngest son thinks that a wombat is a thing you use to play wom.

63. A woman was walking in the park with eleven children following her.

'Good afternoon,' called a friendly gardener. 'Are all the children yours, or is it a picnic.'

'Unfortunately,' replied the woman, 'the children are all mine – and it's certainly no picnic.'

64. Every family should have two children. That way, if one of them becomes a poet or a painter, the other can give them financial support.

65. Yesterday, my young daughter (we called her 'Yesterday' because she was an afterthought) asked my husband: 'Where do I come from?'

He was rather embarrassed, so he told her to ask me.

'Where do I come from?' she asked again, and so I carefully explained to her all about love, marriage, sex, the whole facts of life.

My daughter then said: 'Yes – I know all that. But where do I come from? My friend Sally comes from Cardiff – where do *I* come from?'

66. My daughter walks very quietly whenever she's near the bathroom cabinet. She says she doesn't want to wake the sleeping pills.

67. My small son went with some friends to the local ice rink. When he returned he told me: 'I still don't know if I can skate. I can't seem to stand upright long enough to find out.'

68. I once overheard a small girl talking to one of her friends: 'The way mummies and daddies and teachers are always moaning and complaining I think that's why they're called *groan*-ups.'

69. The young TV interviewer asked the old man: 'Do you have any grandchildren?'

'No,' he replied, 'they're all rather ordinary.'

70. My small son showed me this morning how to make a cigarette lighter. He took most of the tobacco out of it.

71. 'Mum,' asked the small girl, 'do you mind if my exam results are like a submarine?'

'What do you mean?' asked the mother.

'Below C-level.'

72. The house-proud woman gave birth to twins. She kept her house immaculately clean. The kitchen permanently smelt of disinfectant.

The twin's milk bottles were always thoroughly sterilized; their clothes washed in the most powerful of washing powders to remove any germs.

Then, when the twins started to get a bit grumpy and grizzly she asked a friend who had successfully coped with triplets what she should do.

'Oh,' said the friend, 'the twins are probably just teething. Why don't you put your finger in their mouth and . . .'

'What!' shrieked the twins' mother. 'Don't you have to boil the finger first?'

73. When I told my children that I used to be young once, they congratulated me on having such a long memory.

74. The children where I live are so sophisticated that when they write rude words on walls they write them in ancient Greek and Latin.

75. Rebecca was going on safari in Africa with her parents during her summer holiday from school. She had to have the usual round of injections some weeks before her trip.

'Please can you put a plaster on my right arm?' Rebecca asked the nurse.

'Why?' said the nurse. 'You're right handed and so I'm giving you the injections on your left arm. Why do you want a plaster on your right arm?'

'Because,' replied Rebecca, 'I have to go back to school

after you've given me the injections.'

'I know,' said the nurse. 'That's why if you have the plaster over your injection on your left arm the other children at school will know you've had an injection and so will not bang or bump into your left arm.'

'If you knew the children in my school,' said Rebecca, 'you'd know that is *exactly* why I want the plaster on the wrong arm.'

76. It was a tough school. Two girls, Sophie and Susan, were arguing in the playground.

'*My* mother is better than *your* mother,' shouted Sophie.

'And *my* father is better than *your* father,' snapped Susan.

'Oh,' said Sophie. 'I suppose he is. Even my mum says so.'

77. I was sitting on a crowded train from Bournemouth to Waterloo when a young woman with her five children got on at Southampton. The children were all eating ice creams.

The train was so crowded there was nowhere to sit, so they stood in the narrow aisle and one of the children's ice creams kept touching the expensive fur coat of one of the seated passengers.

'Bernard!' snapped the child's mother. 'Don't hold your ice cream like that. You're getting bits of fur stuck in it.'

78. Small girl: 'Mummy, my tummy aches.'

Mother: 'That's because you haven't eaten much – your tummy is empty.'

Small girl: 'So when you had a headache last night was your head empty?'

79. Wilbur had just returned from an overseas business trip and staggered home with a large, brightly wrapped parcel. He was met at the door by his five children.

'Daddy,' asked one of the children, 'what's in the parcel?'

'It's a wonderful new toy,' replied Wilbur. 'It was given to me by one of my firm's clients. The problem is, he only gave me one toy, and as there are five of you, I don't know which one of you should have the toy.'

'Can't we share it?' asked one of the children.

'I suppose you could,' agreed Wilbur, 'but it's something that can only be played with by one person at a time, so I need to work out which one of you gets to use it first. Now, which person in the family always does as Mum tells them and never answers back?'

One of the children immediately responded: 'Daddy, you'd better have first go with the toy, then.'

CHRISTENING
80. When the Mexican fireman had twin sons he had them christened Jose and Hose B.

81. I once knew a couple who wanted their baby to behave during its christening and so they practised every day for a week before the service by using the kitchen sink.

CHRISTMAS
82. Every Christmas I get an awful pain that stays for a week. Then my mother-in-law goes back to her own home.

83. 'Mummy,' said the small boy, 'can I have a saluki or a dachshund for Christmas?'

'No,' replied his mother, 'you'll have what lots of other people are having – turkey.'

84. The little girl would have bought her grandmother a box of handkerchiefs for Christmas, but she couldn't do this as she said she didn't know the exact size of her grandmother's nose.

85. What do angry mice send at Christmas?

Cross mouse cards.

86. I once gave my boyfriend a pocket comb for Christmas, but he never used it. He said he didn't need to comb his pockets.

87. My husband is always moaning at me. Whatever I do, he can find something to complain about.

Last Christmas he gave me two pairs of ear-rings – one covered in plastic pearls and the other in fake diamonds.

When I put on the plastic pearl ones he said: 'What's wrong with the diamond ones? Don't you like them?'

88. I can always tell what my wife is getting me for Christmas by looking at the receipts the credit card company sends to me.

89. 'At Christmas we went to the pantomime. It was *Finderella*.'

'That sounds rather fishy to me.'

'It was. It had a Fairy Codmother in it, and Finderella lost her flipper at the fish ball.'

CHURCH
90. The only times a lot of people go to Church is when they go to see things thrown: water at christenings, confetti and rice at weddings, and earth at funerals.

CINEMA
91. When I go to the cinema I want to be entertained. I want to see adventure stories and comedies. I *don't* want to see sex, violence and bad language – I get all that from my wife.

92. I've given up trying to see a film at the cinema. Last night I bought five separate tickets and *still* I didn't get in to see the film.

Every time I bought a ticket and went towards the film theatre a stupid man took my ticket and tore it in half – so I had to get another one. Then he would do the same to that one, too.

93. 'I know one thing that's always on at the cinema.'
'What's that?'
'The roof.'

CIRCUS
94. The last time I went to a circus there was a man eating penknives. He was a sword swallower on a diet.

CLOTHES
95. I have a dress for every day of the year – and this is it.

COMPUTER DATING
96. I tried computer dating once – but it was a bit disappointing. When I took it to dinner and then a disco the computer didn't have much to say.

CONFERENCES
97. The British businessman was due to address an overseas conference, but his 'plane was delayed and so he had to rush straight from the airport to the conference hotel and then almost immediately had to give his speech.

While he was racing across the hotel's foyer he noticed the public toilets with the symbols of a man and a woman on the appropriate doors. He memorized the wording underneath the symbols.

Thus he began his speech with what he thought was 'Ladies and Gentlemen' in the local language. Unfortunately, his speech was not fully appreciated as he actually began by saying: 'Ladies' toilets and gentlemen's urinals. Welcome to you all.'

CONVERSATIONS
98. The best opener for any conversation is a bottle opener.

99. 'I bet I can make you talk like a Red Indian.'
'How?'
'There you are! I told you I could do it.'

100. I always know if it's a wrong number when my wife answers the 'phone – the conversation only lasts for twenty minutes.

101. My wife loves bitchy gossip – so does her best friend. Whenever they use the 'phone they speak poison to poison.

COWS

102. What theatre shows make cows feel ill?
  Moo-sickals.

103. Where do intelligent cows like to visit on their holidays?
  Moo-seums.

104. How can you stop milk from turning sour?
  Leave it in the cow.

105. Where do cows go for outings?
  To the moo-vies.

106. The reason the cow jumped over the moon is because the new milkmaid had icy cold hands.

107. What game do cows play at parties?
  Moo-sical chairs.

108. What says 'Oom, oom?'
  A backward cow.

109. What is the cow capital of the USA?
  Moo York.

110. Where do you find details of famous cows?
  In *Moo's Who*.

CRUISE
111. My wife and I have recently returned from a luxury cruise. On our first day at sea we received a note from the captain asking us to sit with him at dinner.

We didn't join him as my wife thought it was outrageous that we should pay a small fortune to go on the cruise and then be expected to eat with the staff.

DANCING
112. There's only two things wrong with my husband's dancing – his left foot and his right foot.

DECORATORS
113. When I told the Irish decorators that I wanted a matt finish on the walls they nailed the carpets to them.

DEFINITIONS
114. Apricots: beds for baby apes.

115. Assets: baby donkeys.

116. Booby trap: a bra that is too small and too tight.

117. Derange: de place where de cowboys ride home to.

118. Impale: to put in a bucket.

119. Inkling: a small bottle of ink.

120. Operator: a person who hates opera.

121. Pigtail: a story about a pig.

122. Politics: sounds coming from a parrot that has swallowed a watch.

123. Polymath: a parrot that likes mathematics.

124. Triplets: small journeys.

DENTIST

125. The beautiful young lady in the dentist's chair was nervously wringing her hands. 'Oh dear,' she said, 'I'm so nervous. It's so frightening. I think I'd rather have a baby than my teeth seen to.'

'Well,' replied the dentist, 'which would you like the most – just let me know and I'll adjust the chair – and my clothes – accordingly.'

DIETS

126. When I went on a diet of baked beans and garlic all I lost was one ounce and ten friends.

DIVORCE

127. A friend of mine has just got divorced due to incompatibility. He had no income and his wife had no pat-ability.

128. In olden days England the unfaithful princess was divorced because she had lots of sleepless knights.

129. A couple I used to know recently got divorced and they fought over the custody of their teenage children – neither of them wanted custody.

DOCTOR

130. I tried to follow my doctor's advice and give up smoking cigarettes and try chewing gum instead – but the matches kept getting stuck and the gum wouldn't light.

131. Last week my friend, Mabel, was feeling terribly ill so her husband 'phoned the doctor's surgery.

'I'm afraid the doctor is busy until 10am Thursday,' said the receptionist.

'But that's three days away! My wife is terribly ill,' pleaded Mabel's husband. 'What if she's dead by then?'

'Well,' replied the receptionist, 'you can always 'phone and cancel the appointment.'

132. 'Doctor, doctor! How can I get this ugly mole off my face?'

'Get your dog to chase it back into its hole.'

133. Before I went off to India for my summer holidays I asked my doctor how I could avoid getting a disease from biting insects. He just told me not to bite any.

134. Hospital consultant: 'The woman in that bed is the love of my life.'

Matron: 'Then why haven't you married her?'

Hospital consultant: 'I can't afford to – she's a private patient.'

135. When I asked my doctor to give me something to sharpen my appetite he just gave me a razor blade.

136. When I told the doctor's receptionist that I kept thinking I was a billiard ball she told me to get to the end of the cue.

137. Yesterday I was in the doctor's waiting room and I heard a ninety-six-year-old man pleading with the doctor for a lower sex drive.

'Surely you're imagining things,' said the doctor. 'You're ninety-six years old. Isn't all the feeling for sex just in your head?'

'Yes,' replied the elderly man, 'that's why I want you to lower my sex drive to the place where it might do more good.'

138. Patient: 'Doctor, doctor! I've just swallowed a whole sheep.'

Doctor: 'How do you feel?'

Patient: 'Quite baa-d.'

139. This morning I went to the doctor to see if he had a cure for my wife's sinus trouble. Every time she drags me out shopping she keeps telling me 'sign us' for this, 'sign us' for that.

140. 'Doctor, doctor! My small son has just swallowed a roll of film.'

'Don't worry. Let him rest a bit and we'll wait and see what develops.'

141. Since I had treatment by a private doctor I've lost five kilos in weight. The doctor's bill was so enormous I've been unable to afford to buy any food to eat.

142. Last Tuesday I was in the doctor's waiting room and a young man came in with an expensive watch for the doctor.

'Thank you, thank you, thank you!' said the man, giving the doctor the expensive watch. 'This is a small token of my thanks for all your excellent treatment of my uncle.'

'But he died last week,' said the doctor.

'I know,' replied the young man. 'Thanks to your treatment I've just inherited five million pounds.'

143. What did the vampire doctor shout out in his waiting room?

'Necks please!'

144. Patient: 'Doctor, I want to stop pulling funny faces.'
   Doctor: 'Why?''
   Patient: 'Because the ugly people don't like it when I pull their faces.'

145. When my mother-in-law went to the doctor and complained that her nose runs and her feet smell, he said: 'I'm not surprised. You were made upside down.'

146. The woman went to see the doctor. She had a large flower growing out of the top of her head.

The doctor looked at the flower and said: 'That is quite remarkable. I've never seen anything like that before. But I'll soon cut it off.'

'Cut it off?' snapped the woman. 'I don't want the flower cut off. I just want it treated against greenfly.'

147. While I was in the doctor's waiting room there was this tiny man only about six inches tall. Although he was there before me, he let me see the doctor first. I suppose he just had to be a little patient.

148. 'Doctor, doctor! Can you help me? My tongue keeps sticking out.'

'That's good. Now, if you can just lick these stamps . . .'

149. When the young man was being examined by the doctor he was asked: 'Does it burn when you pee in the toilet?'

'I don't know,' replied the young man, 'I don't think I'd dare hold a match to it.'

150. 'Doctor, doctor! I feel like a piano.'

'Then I'd better take some notes.'

151. I went to the doctor this morning and told him I felt run down.

'Why do you feel that?'' he asked.

'Because,' I replied, 'I've got tyre marks on my legs.'

152. Patient: 'Doctor, every time I eat fruit I get this strange urge to give people all my money.'

Doctor: 'Would you like an apple or a banana?'

153. When the doctor came to visit my aunt Claudette my aunt said: 'Doctor, I hope you're going to tell me that I'm very ill.'

The doctor looked at my aunt and said: 'But why? Don't you want me to say you're very healthy?'

'No,' replied aunt Claudette. 'I feel absolutely terrible. And I don't want to feel like this if I'm healthy. But I'm sure you can make me better.'

DOGS

154. Our house is so small I had to train the dog to wag its tail up and down instead of from side-to-side.

155. One day I'd like to have enough courage to say to people who keep telling me that their pet dog is just like one of the family: 'Oh – which one is it like?'

156. What do you use for measuring the noise a dog makes?

A barking meter.

157. A friend of mine keeps making films about canine creatures – they are all *dog*umentaries.

158. What do you get if you cross a cocker spaniel with a poodle and a cockerel?

A cockerpoddledoo.

159. When Poole and Bournemouth introduced bye-laws to ban dogs from certain parts of the beach and to fine their owners if the dogs fouled public places, a friend of mine decided that she had better train her dog to go to the toilet in the gutter. This was rather difficult, as the dog kept falling off the roof.

160. My dog is a doberman pincher. Every time he sees a doberman he pinches it.

161. I've just come from an awkward meeting with my next-door neighbour. He's almost seven feet tall and has a huge Alsatian dog.

Unfortunately, the dog kept leaping at the garden fence so much that it made a hole in it and got into my garden. That was when it happened. My little cat killed the big Alsatian.

'How did your puny cat kill Big Al, my dog?' demanded my neighbour.

'I'm sorry,' I said, 'but my cat stuck in your dog's throat and he choked to death.'

DRINK

162. I asked my wife to give me a stiff drink and she put starch in my tea.

163. A large man with an enormous beer belly went into his usual pub, asked for a pint of beer, and then took a mirror out of his pocket.

'What are you going to do with the mirror?' asked the barmaid, as the man propped the mirror up on the bar counter.

'Look in it,' replied the man, sipping his pint of beer. 'My doctor told me today that I have to watch my drinking.'

164. At the bar last night was a man who demanded to be served a drink called Less.

'I've never heard of it,' said the barmaid.

'But you *must* have,' insisted the man.

'We don't have it. Is Less a new foreign beer or something? Where did you hear about it?' asked the barmaid.

'I don't exactly know what it is,' replied the man, 'but my doctor insists that I should drink Less.'

DRIVERS

165. When the professor of mathematics was involved in a car crash he was asked by a policeman if he could remember the other car's registration number.

'Not exactly,' replied the professor, 'but the total of the numbers divided by the last digit was equal to the square root of the second number.'

166. I was on a walk in Dorset, lost in thought, when a car pulled up beside me and a fat gentleman wound down his car window and shouted: 'Yokel! Do you know the way to Bournemouth?'

'Yes,' I replied, and continued walking.

167. Policeman: 'I'm arresting you for speeding.'

Angry man: 'Speeding? I can't possibly have been speeding. Why pick on me? Why didn't you stop the people back there instead? I saw they were speeding when I overtook them.'

168. The sports car came hurtling down the narrow, winding country lane, narrowly avoiding an elderly lady in an old car.

'Pig!' shouted the elderly lady as the sports car driver scraped past her car.

'Bitch!' shouted back the sports car driver as he drove on and around the corner – and hit a pig in the middle of the road.

169. Policeman: 'Madam, I have just recorded you as 50 at least.'

Female speeding motorist: 'Don't be ridiculous, officer! These clothes always make me look a lot older.'

DRUNKS

170. The drunk was staggering along the street when he was stopped by a policeman.

'Excuse me, sir,' said the policeman, 'but where are you going?'

'I'm going to a lec . . . lecture,' replied the drunk.

'Who is giving the lecture?' asked the policeman.

'Wh . . . when I . . . when I g . . . get home,' said the drunk, 'my wife will give me the lecture.'

E

ENGLISH

171. The intrepid explorer ventured into the deepest, darkest, most dangerous jungle and eventually came to a small clearing in which a large, middle-aged gentleman sat watching a fire.

'Hello!' said the explorer.

'H . . . sch . . . hello,' replied the middle-aged gentle-man.

'Do you live in a nearby village?' asked the explorer.

'Sch . . . sch . . . yes,' replied the middle-aged gentle-man. 'Sch . . . sch . . . I sush . . . suppose you sch . . . sch . . . must be an sch . . . sch . . . explorer.'

'Yes. You speak very good English. I thought you would only speak the native language. Where did you learn English.'

'Sch . . . sch . . . simple,' replied the middle-aged gentleman. 'Sch . . . sch . . . from . . . sch . . . sch . . . BBC World sch . . . sch . . . service radio.'

F

FARMING
172. I once knew a farmer who, whenever he drove at night, used to drive his car through a stream in order to dip his headlights.

173. Another farmer I know is trying to cross a cow with an octopus. He wants to breed a creature that can milk itself.

FAULTS
174. According to my wife, I've only got two faults – everything I say, and everything I do.

FIRE

175. The house was on fire. A woman appeared at an upstairs window. She was clutching a baby and screaming: 'My baby! My baby! Save my baby!'

'Throw the baby down to me!' shouted a young man. 'I'll catch him.'

'You might drop him,' shouted the woman.

'I'm a professional footballer,' shouted the man 'I'm a goalkeeper. I'm very good at catching. The baby will be safe with me.'

The woman threw down the baby to the young man who put all his professional expertise into operation, and he expertly caught the baby and then, unthinkingly, kicked it over the garden wall.

176. Man on 'phone: 'Help! Come quickly! My house is on fire!'

Fire brigade officer: 'How do we get to your house?'

Man on 'phone: 'What? Don't you still have those big red trucks?'

FISHING

177. Last weekend I did something I've never done before – I went fly fishing: and caught a three ounce fly!

FOOD

178. Barbara: 'I still feel rather sick today.'

Bill: 'Do you know what caused it?'

Barbara: 'I think it must have been the oysters I ate last night.'

Bill: 'Were they bad? What did they look like when you opened them?'

Barbara: 'Oh! You mean you're supposed to *open* them before you eat them?'

179. I once saw a man eat a pocket watch. Then he swallowed two wristwatches. He said I could stay and see him swallow even more watches – but I said I thought it was very time consuming.

180. Rhubarb always seems to look like rather embarrassed celery.

181. 'I'm going to eat a pet,' said the small girl to her brother.

'You can't do that!' protested the brother. 'It's cruel and they will taste horrible.'

'I *am* going to eat a pet,' insisted the sister, defiantly.

The boy was almost in tears as he asked his sister: 'Is it the baby kitten or the puppy you're going to eat?'

'Neither,' replied the sister. 'The pet I'm going to eat is a crumpet!'

FOOTBALL

182. 'Dad, dad!' said Gareth. 'I think I've been selected for the school football team.'

'That's good,' replied Gareth's father. 'But why do you only *think* you've been selected? Aren't you sure? What position will you play?'

'Well,' said Gareth, 'it's not been announced officially, but I overheard the football coach tell my teacher that if I was in the team I'd be a great draw-back.'

183. My wife and son were watching a football match on TV when my son got excited and shouted: 'Pass the ball!

Pass the ball! Why won't the idiot pass the ball to Smith?'

'Well,' said my wife, 'you can't really expect a foot-baller who cost £750,000 to pass the ball to a player who cost a lot less.'

184. When I was a young boy all the other kids insisted that I was in the football team. They said I was vital to the game. They couldn't possibly play without me. They needed me. I was the only one with a football.

FORTUNE TELLING
185. My husband wanted his fortune told, but didn't know whether to go to a mindreader or a palmist. I told him to go to a palmist – at last we know he's got a palm.

186. 'I've heard that you are an excellent fortune teller. Can you predict the next few months?'

'Certainly! December, January, February.'

G

GARDENING
187. My wife, Virginia, likes to talk to the plants in the garden. So far, only one of them talks back and is always saying things like: 'You're wonderful, beautiful. Thank you for looking after me in the garden. You're fantastic!'

I suppose this was only to be expected of a plant called Virginia Creeper!

188. What is the favourite flower of a pet frog?
A croakus.

GHOSTS
189. Where do ghosts take their dirty coats?
To a dry-screamers.

190. What did the phantom on guard duty outside the haunted castle say when he heard a noise?
'Halt! Who ghosts there?'

191. Why was the shy ghost frightened of going to the opticians' party?
Because he thought he might make a spooktacle of himself.

192. It was a graveyard romance. Boy meets ghoul.

193. What music do ghosts like?
Haunting melodies.

194. How did the two ghosts fall in love?
It was love at first fright.

195. On what day do ghosts play tricks on each other?
April Ghoul's Day.

196. Where can you catch a ghost train?
At a manifestation.

197. Why did the female ghoul like demons?
Because demons are a ghoul's best friend.

198. What do you call a female ghost who serves drinks and food on a 'plane?

An air ghostess.

199. Some years ago I tried to become a ghost writer. But I couldn't find any ghosts who wanted me to write for them.

GIRLFRIENDS

200. My girlfriend can never understand why her brother has five sisters and she only has four.

201. My new girlfriend is like a grapefruit. Whenever I squeeze her she spits at me.

202. 'I thought you said your new girlfriend was a model? With the greatest of respect, she doesn't really look like one. What does she model?'

'Halloween masks.'

203. My girlfriend is a real sex object. Whenever I mention sex she objects.

204. I asked another girl I went out with if she liked nuts, and she replied: 'Why? Do you want me to marry you?'

205. My girlfriend says she only weighs eight stones – but I reckon the stones must be the size of boulders.

206. My girlfriend is one of twins. It would be quite difficult to tell them apart – if my girlfriend didn't have a moustache.

207. When someone asked my girlfriend if she ever had much trouble making up her mind, she said: 'I'm not sure. Maybe yes. Maybe no.'

208. This morning I bought my girlfriend a sexy new nightdress. Tonight I'll try and talk her out of it.

209. My girlfriend speaks Italian like a native – a native from Scunthorpe.

210. I'll never forget my first girlfriend. It was real puppy love. Every time I went to kiss her she said 'Woof!'

GOAT

211. I once knew a man who thought he was a goat. He'd believed that ever since he was a young kid.

GOLF

212. Mrs. Brown was fed up with her husband being forever out of the house and playing golf.

'Why can't you stay at home a bit more?' she asked.

'Because it's fun on the golf course,' replied her husband. 'And it's good exercise.'

'Maybe I should try it, too?' suggested Mrs. Brown.

'You probably wouldn't like it,' said Mr. Brown. 'All the walking might tire you out. Why don't you stay at home with your TV and the knitting?'

But Mrs. Brown insisted her husband took her to the golf club and gave her lessons.

The very first day together on the course, her husband's first shot was appalling, but he told his wife: 'There!

That's how to hit the ball. Another two or three strokes and that'll be it.'

Mrs. Brown then took her first ever shot – and scored a hole in one.

Mr. Brown was amazed. He was speechless.

The couple walked over to where the ball nestled in the hole and Mrs. Brown said: 'That wasn't very good, was it? It's going to be very difficult to hit the ball out of this little hole.'

HARD TIMES

213. Lord and Lady Dross-Plott had fallen on hard times.

'We must make some economies,' said the Lord. 'Couldn't you have some cookery lessons? Then you could do all our meals and we wouldn't have to continue employing the cook.'

'Only if you would have some lessons, too,' replied Lady Dross-Plott. 'If you had some sex lessons then I wouldn't need the butler and we could dispense with him, too.'

HOLIDAY

214. The young man was on his first ever holiday abroad. As he lay on the beach in a crowded part of Spain, a gorgeous young woman lay down beside him and kept making admiring glances at him.

Eventually, she said: 'I like the look of you. Would you like to come back to my apartment for a little game?'

'Fantastic!' replied the young man. 'I was just wondering where I'd find a snooker table.'

215. Mother, in holiday apartment: 'Sarah, can you wash up the dishes.'

Sarah: 'But we don't have any rubber gloves. You know water isn't very good for my skin.'

Mother: 'Is that why you've spent most of the day in the sea?'

216. Mr. and Mrs. Smith and Mr. and Mrs. Brown had known each other for many years and frequently went on holiday together.

This year Mr. Smith suggested to Mr. Brown that to add spice to their holiday, perhaps they should exchange partners. Mr. Brown considered this for a moment, then agreed it was a good idea, and both men got their wives to agree, too.

Thus it was that after their first night in Malta, Mr. Brown turned to his holiday partner in bed and said: 'That was certainly exciting and different.'

'Yes, I agree,' said his partner, Mr. Smith.

HORSES
217. What game do horses like to play?

Stable tennis.

HOSPITAL
218. I've just come out of hospital. I was in there for six weeks as a result of my boyfriend throwing me over. He

caught me out with another man and threw me over a cliff.

219. Frederick's wife was a surgeon, and so when Frederick had to go into hospital for an operation, she insisted on doing the surgery. She said she didn't want anyone else to open her male.

220. Bernard was walking along the street one day when a young man rushed up to him and said: 'Can you show me the quickest way to get to the hospital?'

So Bernard pushed the young man under a bus.

221. There I was, lying ill in hospital, and my husband came into the room to read to me – my insurance policies and last will and testament.

222. A friend of mine recently went into hospital for an organ transplant. Now his body can play all the hymns in the church.

HOTELS

223. Hotel receptionist: 'Would you like a room with a private bath?'

Young man: 'That's all right, I'm not shy. I don't mind who sees me. The bath doesn't *have* to be private.'

224. A man arrived at an hotel in a large conference town.

'Do you have a room for the night?' he asked.

'I'm sorry,' said the receptionist, 'but we are fully booked. All the other hotels are probably full, too.'

'But surely,' said the man, 'you must be able to find

some room somewhere? Suppose I was Prince Charles in
disguise – surely you'd find a room for him?'

'Yes, we would,' admitted the receptionist.

'Well,' said the man, 'as Prince Charles isn't coming,
please can I have his room?'

225. My hotel is so noisy I couldn't sleep at all last night.

I complained to the hotel manager and said I had
specifically requested a quiet room. He said the *room* was
quiet – it was the traffic outside, the lift next to it, and the
people in all the other rooms that were noisy.

226. There were three conventions going on all at the
same time and so when I arrived all the hotels were full.

'Surely you've had a cancellation?' I said to the
receptionist at the biggest hotel. 'Surely there's a room for
me somewhere?'

'I'm sorry,' replied the receptionist, 'but all the rooms
are booked.'

'Isn't there perhaps another single man who is in a twin-
bedded room and who might like to share the cost of the
room?' I asked.

'Well,' said the receptionist, 'Mr. Jones was forced to
take a twin-bedded room three nights ago because no
singles were available, and he did moan about the cost of
it all, and he did share the room last night with another
gentleman. But that gentleman found it most uncomfort-
able and quit.'

'Why?' I enquired.

'It would appear that Mr. Jones has a snore that is
louder than the noise of an electric saw or an aeroplane
taking off.'

'That's all right,' I replied. 'I don't mind sharing with
Mr. Jones.'

So I was introduced to Mr. Jones, he agreed to share his room with me, and I had a peaceful and pleasant night's sleep.

The next day the receptionist asked me: 'Did you sleep well?'

'Very well,' I replied.

The receptionist raised her eyebrows in slight astonishment, and asked: 'Did you use ear-plugs?'

'No,' I said. 'But when it was time to go to bed, I gave Mr. Jones a sloppy wet kiss on his cheek, called him a gorgeous hunk of a man – and I think he spent the rest of the night sitting up wide awake and in panic, watching me.'

HOUSES

227. I've stopped living in a house. I now live in a kennel. My kids made all my books dog-eared, my wife treats me like a dog, and all my work makes me dog-tired – so I might as well stay in the kennel.

228. What clothes does a house wear?
Address.

229. I used to live in a house in Llanfighangel-Tal-y-llyn in Wales – but I had to move because I couldn't spell the address.

HUSBANDS

230. For twenty-two years my husband and I were happy – then we met and got married.

231. My husband used to be a professional violinist, but he had to give it up because it gave him a bad back. It was

all the bending down to pick up the coins in the hat that
did it . . .

232. My husband was such an ugly baby that his mother
refused to push him in his pram – she pulled it.

233. I think I have the perfect husband. Pity I'm not
married to him.

234. My husband has more chins than the Hong Kong
'phone book.

235. My husband is so stupid that when I gave birth to
triplets he wanted to know who the other two fathers
were.

236. My husband doesn't really have a big mouth – but he
once gave the kiss of life to a whale.

237. Someone once asked me if I believed in clubs for
promiscuous husbands. I said that poison was safer than
using a club.

238. My husband has got a memory like an elephant – and
a face to match.

239. My husband is so pedantic, if you say to him 'How
do you do?', he'll reply: 'Do what?'

240. My sister has just lost two hundred pounds of ugly
fat – her husband left her.

241. My husband has finally given up eating Smarties. He said it took too long to peel off the shells to get to the chocolate.

242. My husband's cooking is so bad he's even managed to give the dustbin food poisoning.

243. My husband keeps pining for his lost youth – he lost her to another boy at school.

244. Last year the children and I had a lot of fun on holiday burying my husband in the sand on the beach. Next year we might go back and dig him up.

245. My husband is so stupid, when I told him the car battery was dead he took it out and buried it.

246. When my husband told me that his pot belly had got a lot smaller, I told him it was only wishful shrinking.

247. I know my husband's hair is all his own – I went with him when he made the final payment on his wig.

248. I have a special soft spot for my husband – a large swamp in Africa.

249. I don't know what to make of my husband. I suppose if I was a cannibal I could make him into a casserole.

250. My sister has had five husbands – two of her own, and three married to friends.

251. I like to make my husband laugh on New Year's Day so I tell him jokes on Boxing Day.

252. Last year when I was on holiday in the USA I bought a lovely chair for my husband. Now all I've got to do is plug it in.

253. Overheard conversation: 'Don't you mind your husband chasing after pretty young women?'

'Not really. It's a bit like dogs chasing after cars – they wouldn't know what to do if they caught one.'

254. Fred came home early from work one day and found his wife in bed with the postman.

'What on earth do you think you're doing?' demanded Fred.

'I see what you mean,' said the postman to Fred's wife, continuing his exertions. 'He really is as stupid as you said he is, if he has to ask a question like that!'

I

INSURANCE
255. My wife is so silly she thinks a lump sum insurance policy only pays out if she gets lumps.

INTRODUCTIONS
256. Our next speaker really ought to be called Money – because he truly fulfils that old saying: 'When Money talks, everyone listens.'

257. He's a comedian with a way-out sense of humour. Whenever he tells a joke in the theatre, people ask for the way out.

258. Now we have a magician who dipped his top hat and magic wand in some mud just before he came to the theatre – so now he can show us some dirty tricks.

259. Now we have a country singer. He has to sing in the country as they don't want him in the town.

260. Next we have a singer who can charm the birds out of the trees – vultures, crows, buzzards . . .

261. Now we have a man with many hidden talents. One day he might find them.

262. Next we have someone who is rapidly becoming a star – already her head comes to a point.

263. Our next speaker has just flown in from Hollywood where he has appeared in a number of pictures – he wouldn't get out of the way when all the Japanese tourists were taking photos.

264. Our next performer is a musician who has just worked out the difference between his brass and his oboe.

INVESTMENTS
265. Are stockbrokers so called because they sell you stock that makes you broke?

266. With so much uncertainty in the Stock Market, many investors are no longer bulls or bears – they're chickens or lemmings.

267. A friend once asked me for some investment advice. I asked him if he had any liquid assets. He said he did – three bottles of Scotch and a can of fizzy orange.

ITALY
268. I didn't have much trouble speaking Italian when I was on holiday in Italy – it was just that the Italians seemed to have trouble understanding it.

269. I once went on a tour of Rome. Our tour party was being shown around one of the historic sites and the guide said: 'This ancient statue dates back more than 2,000 years.'

'Don't be silly,' said one of the tourists, 'it's only 1991 now.'

270. I was standing in a queue in a hamburger restaurant the other day when I overheard two girls talking. One girl was blonde, the other brunette.

'Did you manage to pick up any Italian when you were on holiday in Rome?' asked the blonde.

'Yes,' replied the brunette. 'Lots.'

'Let's hear some,' asked the blonde.

'Well,' replied the brunette, 'they all spoke almost perfect English.'

J

JAPANESE

271. I once knew a Japanese gentleman who was so wealthy that he was considering buying himself what he called 'a place down South'. It was Australia.

JOBS

272. The young student was desperate for money and so in his vacation he decided to take a job in a local factory as it paid good wages.

'Now,' said the supervisor, 'your first job is to sweep the floor.'

'But I've got a BA degree,' said the student, 'and I'm currently studying for a masters in business administration.'

'Oh!' said the supervisor. 'In that case I'd better show you how to hold the broom.'

273. My job is very secure – it's *me* they can do without.

274. When I left university I went for several job interviews. At the first interview I was turned down because I wasn't married. The personnel officer said that married men had much more experience of knowing how to cope if a boss shouted at them.

275. Sarah has just changed her job due to men trouble. There weren't any men in her office.

276. My wife is thinking of applying for a job as a

telephone canvasser – she says she'll enjoy making little tents for telephones.

277. A friend of mine is very pleased with his wife. He thinks she's got a good part-time job with a London Law firm, working two evenings each week. But all she told him was that to get money for a few extra luxuries, she would now be soliciting in Paddington.

278. My sister has a very responsible job. If anything goes wrong, she's responsible.

279. The best job for people who think they are paranoid is driving a taxi – then they really will always have people talking behind their backs.

280. I was once interviewing people for a job as my secretary, and when I asked one girl how many words she could type per minute, she replied: 'Well, it depends if they are long words or short words. But I can erase at eighty words a minute.'

KNITTING
281. My wife was knitting the most peculiar garment last week. It had lots of strings at the top and a huge canopy. She said it was a parachute jumper.

KNOCK, KNOCK

282. 'Knock, knock.'
  'Who's there?'
  'Luke.'
  'Luke who?'
  'Luke through the keyhole and you'll see who.'

283. 'Knock, knock.'
  'Who's there?'
  'Who.'
  'Who who?'
  'Sorry, I don't talk to owls.'

284. 'Knock, knock.'
  'Who's there?'
  'Cook.'
  'Cook who?'
  'Oh, I didn't know it was Spring already.'

285. 'Knock, knock.'
  'Who's there?'
  'Mary.'
  'Mary who?'
  'Mary Christmas and a Happy New Year.'

286. 'Knock, knock.'
  'Who's there?'
  'Hatch.'
  'Hatch who?'
  'Bless you!'

L

LAND

287. I once knew a man who was sold a plot of land at the North Pole. He thought it was the ideal place to grow frozen peas.

LAW

288. If it is the law of gravity that keeps us from falling off the Earth as it zooms around the Sun, what kept us on Earth before the law was passed?

289. 'Now,' said the prosecution counsel to the lady in the witness box, 'at the time of the car crash, what gear were you in?'

'Umm,' mused the lady, 'I think it was blue jeans and a tight white T-shirt.'

290. The complicated commercial lawsuit had dragged on for years and years.

'I've had enough of this,' said the managing director of one of the firms involved. 'Let's come to a compromise solution and settle out of court.'

'Impossible!' snorted the City solicitor. 'My firm is determined to fight your case right down to your last penny.'

291. The slowest writers are in prison. They can sometimes spend more than twenty years on one sentence.

292. The criminal who stole a ton of rubber bands was given a long stretch.

293. The defendant in one court case said that at the time the crime was committed he was in hospital recovering from a vicious attack by a shark while swimming in the sea: he therefore had a water-bite alibi.

294. The solicitor died and went to the gates of Heaven where he was to be interviewed by St. Peter to see if he should be let into Heaven or sent down to Hell.

'I don't know why I died so young,' said the solicitor. 'It doesn't seem fair. I'm only 35.'

'I know,' replied St. Peter. 'But according to all the time you've billed your clients for, you're at least 208!'

295. What is the difference between a law court and an ice making machine?

One gives justice, and the other gives just ice.

296. The man had been arrested and charged with stealing five hundred cigars.

He consulted a solicitor for advice.

'It will probably cost at least two hundred pounds to defend you,' said the solicitor.

'Two hundred pounds!' exclaimed the young man. 'I can't afford that. I'm innocent. I'm *not* guilty! Wouldn't you take a cheque for £20 and a few hundred cigars instead?'

297. Amanda Guv dyed her hair blonde when she became a policewoman so that when she made an arrest people could genuinely say: 'It's a fair cop, Guv.'

298. 'Do you plead guilty or not guilty?'
'Don't I have any other choices?'

299. Why were the police not surprised when Bo Peep lost her sheep?
Because she admitted she had a crook with her.

300. The most difficult task a young lawyer ever had was the evening he spent trying to change a beautiful young lady's will.

301. Albert had just been found guilty of killing his very bossy and argumentative wife by pushing her out of the window of a room on the 29th floor of an hotel.
'This is a very serious offence,' said the judge. 'If your wife had fallen on someone there could have been a very nasty accident.'

302. Why did the policeman arrest three turnips?
Because they were together in a garden plot.

303. 'Members of the jury, have you reached your verdict?'
'Yes we have, your honour. We find the gorgeously sexy woman who stole the jewellery not guilty.'

304. 'Thank you for winning the case,' said the grateful client to her solicitor. He had won her £10,000 from the local council as she had tripped over an uneven paving slab on the pavement and injured her leg.
'It was a pleasure,' said the solicitor, handing the client his bill.
The client took the bill, then frowned: 'This bill is pretty steep. Is it right?'

'Of course,' replied the solicitor. 'It represents good value for all our time, care, experience, expertise and legal knowledge. If it wasn't for us, you wouldn't have won the case.'

'But your costs are almost half the damages,' replied the client. 'If it wasn't for me, you wouldn't have had a case.'

'But,' said the solicitor, 'anyone can trip over a paving slab.'

M

MAIDS

305. The gorgeous new maid had once been a gymnast in Romania. She was now trying to improve her English by working for Lord and Lady Spiffleburgson at their mansion in Dorset.

The maid had been with the Spiffleburgsons for only nine days and found many English habits rather strange. But she was determined to succeed as she desperately needed her salary to help support her family in Romania.

Thus it was that at a luncheon party at the mansion she walked in carefully carrying a large bowl of salad – but the guests were rather astonished that she was completely naked.

The gentlemen at the luncheon raised their eyebrows while secretly admiring her trim, lithe young body, while the ladies demurely tried to look away.

After the maid had placed the bowl of salad on the table and was leaving the room, Lady Spiffleburgson rose from her chair and accompanied the maid to the kitchen.

'My dear,' said her ladyship, 'why are you walking about naked?'

'I only obey your orders,' said the maid. 'I hear you say – you say several times – and you say it important for me to remember – I must serve salad without dressing.'

306. The Browns were a wealthy middle-aged couple who lived in a large house in the country. All went well for many years until a new maid arrived. She was extremely attractive. Within six months of her arrival, Mr. Brown was starting to wake up every morning at 5 a.m. instead of his usual 7.30 a.m.

'Where are you going?' Mrs. Brown would ask, as her husband got out of bed and slipped on his dressing gown.

'Once awake, I can't get back to sleep,' Mr. Brown replied, 'so I think I'll do some work in my study or walk around the garden. You don't need to get up – just go back to sleep. You know how deep sleep keeps you beautiful.'

Mrs. Brown began to suspect that her husband was sneaking into the maid's room. What should she do?

It was soon to be the maid's parents' wedding anniversary, so one Thursday afternoon when Mr. Brown was on a business trip to London, Mrs. Brown suggested that the maid might like to pay a surprise visit to her parents.

'You can go now, if you like,' suggested Mrs. Brown, 'and come back on Monday.'

'Thanks very much,' said the maid, 'it's most kind of you.' And she went off to pack for her trip.

Soon the maid had left the house. Mr. Brown returned around 9 p.m. and, after watching TV for a bit, went to bed.

Promptly at 5 a.m., Mr. Brown woke up and said he couldn't sleep any more and was going for a stroll around the garden.

As soon as her husband left the room, and she could hear him cleaning his teeth in the bathroom, Mrs. Brown rushed to the maid's room and got into the maid's bed.

Mrs. Brown had been lying in the dark for about five minutes when she heard the sash window of the room being slowly lifted and a man climbed in through the window.

Mrs. Brown tensed herself in the darkness, but relaxed as the man made tender, passionate love to her. She was ecstatic. Why could her husband make such wonderful love to the maid and be so boring in bed with her?

'Darling,' whispered Mrs. Brown, snuggling up to the man in bed, 'let's do it again.'

'Sorry, luv,' replied the man. Mrs. Brown was aghast. It was not her husband's voice. 'No time for more now,' continued the man, 'but I can come back when I've finished the milk round.'

MARRIAGE

307. After we got married, I no longer had buttons missing from my shirts, and my clothes were no longer creased – my wife taught me how to sew and iron!

308. They were a well-matched couple as both of them were madly in love – she with herself, and he with himself.

309. My sister has just married for the fourth time. Her first husband was very wealthy. Her second husband was a theatrical producer and she wanted to be in one of his musicals. Her third husband liked donkeys – and she'd always wanted a donkey. And her current husband is Japanese and likes playing a game for two.

In fact, as far as husbands go, she's had one for the money, two for the show, three to get neddy, and four to play Go!

310. The only reason Henrietta married Archibald is because he gave her an engagement ring, then she grew too fat to be able to get it off her finger and give it back to him.

311. People keep saying that two can live as cheaply as one – but they never seem to finish the sentence: one *what*?

312. My girlfriend was so surprised when I asked her to marry me, she almost pushed me out of the bed.

313. I was sitting on a train to London the other day when I overheard two young girls talking.

One girl said: 'Last night, Julian told me that he wanted to marry the cleverest, most beautiful girl in the world.'

'Oh,' replied the other girl, 'that's a pity. He's been your boyfriend for at least two years and now he says he's going to marry someone else.'

314. I married my wealthy husband because he said if I did he would be humbly grateful. Instead, he's been grumbly hateful.

315. I married my husband because I thought he was rich. He said he owned a chain of newspapers.

The day after we married, he took me up to the attic of his mother's house and showed me what he did when he was a small boy at school – made a chain out of old newspapers.

316. For the whole of the first week of our marriage my wife went to bed every night wearing a white glove on her left hand, and a small white sock on her left foot. I thought this was rather odd, but didn't like to ask her about it until the second week I eventually plucked up courage.

'Darling,' said my demure bride, 'my mother said that if I wanted a long and happy marriage I should keep an air of mystery and never let you see me completely naked.'

317. I once knew a man who was so mean he spent years and years before he found his ideal wife – a woman born on 29th February so he would only have to buy her a birthday card every four years.

318. I can marry anyone I please. Trouble is, I haven't pleased anyone yet.

MEETINGS

319. The best time to have an executive meeting is at 4.45 p.m. on a Friday before a Bank Holiday Monday. That way everyone will be keen to get the meeting over with quickly so they can get away for the long weekend and they won't waste time arguing over policy.

MICE

320. What is it when a mouse cleans your home for you?
   Mousework.

321. What game do mice like to play?
   Hide and squeak.

MINING

322. My wife is in the mining business – she's always saying: 'That's mine! That's mine! And that's mine!'

MISERS

323. An elderly miser was passing an undertakers when he noticed that they were having a 'cut price funeral' offer – so he went in and ordered one, then went home and committed suicide.

324. The mean lady was walking along the High Street when an unemployed young man begged her for money.

'I'm homeless, jobless, and I'm starving,' said the man. 'Please give me a few pounds for some soup.'

'A bowl of soup doesn't cost a few pounds,' snapped the lady.

'I know,' said the young man, 'but I have to give the waiter a good tip.'

MONEYLENDER

325. A woman went to the moneylender with a twenty pound note in one ear, and a fifty pound note in the other – she was seventy pounds in arrears ('er ears)!

N

NATIVES

326. There I was on the beach on the far off paradise

island when suddenly I was surrounded by a horde of shouting natives.

They moved in closer and closer and their shouts grew louder and their gestures grew more menacing and dramatic – so I had to give in and buy a cheap necklace and a gaudy T-shirt.

NEWSPAPERS

327. I recently read a newspaper report of a survey that stated that one per cent of males liked women with fat thighs, six per cent preferred ladies with thin thighs – all the rest liked something in between.

328. The politician was on a fact-finding mission overseas and, when he arrived at the airport of one small country, he was greeted by a jostling crowd of newspaper reporters.

'Have you come to see the brothels?' asked one reporter.

The politician was temporarily stunned. Then, not wanting to offend, asked politely: 'Are there any brothels here?'

The next day there were banner headlines in the newspaper: VISITING POLITICIAN ASKS: 'ARE THERE ANY BROTHELS?'

329. I read in the newspaper today that a lot of people have recently been attacked at night and bitten just above the knee. Police are looking for a dwarf vampire.

330. What newspaper do cats read?
The Mews Of The World.

NIGHTCLUBS

331. When the nightclub singer asked me if he sang in the right key, I said he sang more like a monkey.

332. Overheard in a dimly lit nightclub: 'Do you know the difference between sex and conversation?'
　'No.'
　'Then why not come back to my apartment and lie down while I talk to you?'

333. My boyfriend takes me to all the best nightclubs – maybe one day they'll let us in.

334. I recently went to a nightclub where the dance floor was so crowded that when one of the dancers fainted it was half an hour before he could fall down.

NURSE

335. The nurse broke off her engagement to Bernard as she felt she had been deceived.
　Bernard had told her that they had a lot in common as he frequently had to deal with poor hearts and livers. She thought he was a doctor – now she's found out he works in a butcher's shop.

OFFICE

336. When I arrived for work this morning, my secretary

said: 'I can see you've had another quarrel with your wife.'

'Oh,' I said, rather stunned. 'How did you know that?'

'Because,' she replied, 'the kitchen knife is still stuck in your back.'

337. The young secretary, Dawn, used to tell such long, complicated and involved jokes to her colleagues in the office that they were often to be found asleep at the crack of Dawn.

338. I once said to my delightful young secretary: 'I just don't know what to do. What can I give to a valued client – a man who has expensive cars, an art collection worth millions, homes in London, Dorset, Switzerland, Hong Kong and the USA. He's a man with just about everything. What can I possibly give him?'

My secretary looked at me, smiled, and said: 'You're welcome to give him my 'phone number.'

339. My new secretary seems to think that all my correspondence is private and confidential: all the letters she types look as if she's taken them down in shorthand and typed them while wearing a blindfold.

340. Mavis, the office manager, was away on a training course when one of her colleagues enquired: 'What's happened to Mavis?'

Her secretary replied: 'She's abroad.'

'I know,' replied the colleague. 'But I want to know *where* she is, not *what* she is!'

341. Why do I have to work so much overtime at the office?

Because I owe, I owe, so off to work I go.

342. The young office girl was about to get married. Her colleagues made a collection and bought her a wedding present.

'Where shall we hide it until the boss can present it to her?' asked one of her colleagues.

Just then the boss appeared. 'I heard that,' he said. 'Just put the present in a filing cabinet – she never seems capable of finding anything in there!'

343. My new secretary seems to like wearing clothes that bring out the bust in her.

OPERATIONS

344. My wife recently asked me if it was possible for a six-year-old boy to perform heart transplant operations.

'Of course it's not possible,' I replied.

'Jonathan,' shouted my wife. 'Daddy says you can't possibly do the operations. So go and put the hearts back right now!'

P

PARTIES

345. I once went to an important business dinner party and was listening to an interesting conversation between two people at the far end of the table when the host (my boss) passed me a note.

I had forgotten to bring my spectacles, so I handed the note to the man on my right and asked him if he would be kind enough to read me the note as without my spectacles I find it difficult even to read newspaper headlines.

The man looked at the note and read: 'Please talk to the man on your right. He's a long-winded bore, full of his own self-importance and is rather stupid – but we're hoping to pick up a good order from his firm.'

346. Whenever I go to fancy dress parties I always go as Napoleon. That way, I can keep one hand on my wallet.

347. There I was at the office cocktail party. I'd spent a small fortune on a new suit and my wife had spent even more on her dress.

I wanted to impress my new boss, but my wife seemed to be letting me down. Every five minutes or so she would go over to the bar and get a drink and bring it back to where I was standing, and then rapidly drink it with her back to the bar.

By the time she had finished her seventh drink I noticed that my boss was watching her as she made her way back to the bar.

I wanted to go after my wife, but it was difficult to break off the conversation I was having with someone from the computer systems department. Out of the corner of my eye I could see my boss talking to my wife. He smiled. She smiled. He frowned. Then she walked back to me.

'Darling,' I said to my wife, when the computer systems man had moved on to buttonhole someone else, 'what did my boss say to you? Did he comment on all the drinks you've had? That won't do my career much good. He must think you've got a drink problem.'

'No he doesn't,' replied my wife. 'He certainly doesn't think I've got a drink problem. I'm *not* a liability to you, darling. I simply told him you just keep sending me to the bar to get more drinks for you.'

PASSPORTS

348. When my husband complained that his new passport photo didn't do him justice, I told him that he didn't really want justice – he needed mercy.

349. When you look just like your passport photo you know you're really too sick to travel.

PETS

350. What do you call a plump pet cat that has eaten a duck?

A duck-filled fatty puss.

351. I once knew an Irishman who named his pet zebra 'Spot'.

352. When I was six I was given a goldfish as a pet. Unfortunately, I had to wait until I was seven before I got a bowl to put it in.

PHILOSOPHY

353. Philosophy of a skunk: I stink, therefore I am.

PICNIC

354. For the summer Saturday outing to the park, the

little girl put a small furry animal into a wicker basket – it was her picnic hamster.

PIES

355. 'Dad, can pies fly?'

'No, of course not, son.'

'But mum insists that there are two magpies flying around the garden.'

PIGEON RACING

356. One of my cousins says he wants to take up pigeon racing – but I'm sure he'll never win against them unless he learns how to fly.

'PLANE TRAVEL

357. I was on a 'plane the other day, sitting next to an elderly woman who was on her first 'plane flight.

Just before take-off, the stewardess came round with some boiled sweets and explained to the elderly woman that the sweets would help to reduce the pressure in her ears.

Half an hour after take-off, the elderly woman asked the stewardess if it was now all right to take the sweets out of her ears.

358. I was on a 'plane from Moscow to New York when a man got up from a seat a few rows behind me and began to walk down the aisle towards the toilets and the front of the 'plane.

He looked rather menacing. He was wearing scruffy jeans and a bulky leather jacket which was firmly zipped up. His hands were in his jacket pockets.

Suddenly, he stopped. He looked to where I was sitting and said: 'Hijack.'

I was terrified. He said the word again, even louder: 'Hijack!'

Then the man sitting next to me put down the copy of *Share Millions* he was reading, looked up at the man in the aisle, and said: 'Hi George. How are you? I didn't know you were on this 'plane, too.'

359. As the 'plane flew over the sea I saw something large, black and hairy in the water. It was an oil wig.

PLUMBERS
360. I think my three young sons are going to be plumbers when they grow up – they never come when they're called.

POET
361. A friend of mine is a poet and he's almost starving. He says that rhyme doesn't pay.

POLITICS
362. When a politician says he's 100% behind you, he usually forgets to mention he's also holding a knife.

363. I understand that they are going to erect a huge statue in Trafalgar Square of ———— (insert the name of your own least favourite politician). They are doing it so the pigeons can express the views of us all.

364. Why is it that lunatics and criminals are not allowed to vote – but you *are* allowed to vote for *them*?

365. A relative of mine, Andrew, once went canvassing on behalf of the Labour Party.

The first door he knocked on was opened by a formidable-looking lady with a piercing voice. Seeing Andrew's Labour rosette, the lady launched into a tirade of abuse about the Labour Party, its leaders, MPs, and supporters. 'Utter trash, the lot of them!' she snorted. 'And their policies – if they can ever find them and follow them – stink. Absolute garbage!'

The lady was about to shut the door when Andrew said, rather meekly: 'Does that mean you won't be voting Labour?'

366. Someone once said that politicians stand for whatever the people will fall for.

367. Did you hear about the Conservative MP who, when drunk, revealed such terrifying views to a journalist that he was dumped by his local party organization, ostracized by his former friends, and had to go and live in Australia?

He is now a far off terror Tory.

POLO
368. The reason I don't play polo is because I think it must be incredibly difficult to ride a horse while using a stick to hit little mints.

PRIVATE DETECTIVE
369. I used to be a private detective. I once had to follow

a woman from London to Bournemouth, where she gave me the slip.

Another time I managed to follow her to Newcastle, where she again gave me the slip.

Then I followed her to London where she gave me the slip.

Then I got lucky. When I followed her to York she not only gave me the slip – but her bra and panties, too!

PROMOTION
370. When Simpkins-Smutterwhite was promoted above me – even though I had been with the company for much longer, had more experience and worked much harder than he did – I was not upset. I went straight up to him and said: 'Congratulations! Let me shake you by the throat.'

PSYCHIATRIST
371. The young woman was visiting the male psychiatrist for the first time, and he decided to test her reactions to different pictures.

First, he held up a card on which had been drawn two circles that almost touched.

'What does this make you think of?' asked the psychiatrist.

'Two fat people about to make love,' replied the young woman.

The psychiatrist showed the woman a picture of two wavy lines.

'That looks like the sand on the beach after two people have made passionate love for hours – or maybe it's a waterbed rocking in motion to some lovers in action.'

'Hmm,' said the psychiatrist, leaning back in his chair.

'You seem to be overly pre-occupied with sex.'

'How dare you!' snapped the woman. 'It was *you* that showed me the sexy pictures.'

PUBLIC TELEPHONES

372. There I was, stranded in a strange town, and I urgently needed to use the public telephone.

Unfortunately, a rather plump lady was busily flipping through the pages of the 'phone book and so I could not get to the 'phone.

I waited patiently. Still the plump lady scanned the pages of the 'phone book.

After ten minutes, I grew a little exasperated (it's a small flower related to the tulip) and gently tapped the plump lady on the shoulder.

'Excuse me,' I said. 'Can I help you find a number in the 'phone book?'

'Oh,' she replied. 'I'm not exactly looking for a number. My daughter is expecting her first child next month and she's asked me to suggest some names for it. That's why I'm looking in the 'phone book – to see if I can find some nice-sounding names to suggest.'

QUESTIONS

373. What do you get if you cross a chicken with a clock?
  An alarm cluck.

374. What two letters of the alphabet hurt teeth?
D.K.

375. Who are the two largest females in the USA?
Mrs. Sippi and Miss Ouri.

376. What do elves and pixies have to do when they come home from school?
Gnomework.

377. What tiles are the most difficult to fix to the bathroom wall?
Reptiles.

378. What are the babies of Indian squaws called?
Squawkers.

379. What was the largest moth in the world?
A mam-moth.

380. Why did the singer gargle with soup?
Because she was a souprano.

381. Where do frogs fly their flags?
From tad poles.

382. What gets wetter the more it dries?
A towel.

383. Why did the baby pig eat so much food?
So it could make a hog of itself.

384. What did the skunk do in church?
It sat in a phew.

385. What is the difference between an oak tree and a very tight shoe?

One makes acorns – the other makes corns ache.

386. What slithers along the ground and works for the Government?

A civil serpent.

387. What ring can never be round?

A boxing ring.

388. Where did the major-general keep his armies?

Up his sleevies.

389. What fish races through the water at ninety miles an hour?

A motor pike.

390. What do you call an egg in the middle of the jungle?

An eggsplorer.

391. Which side of a sheep has the most wool?

The outside.

392. What walks about saying: 'ouch, ouch, ouch, ouch, ouch, ouch, ouch, ouch'?

An octopus wearing shoes that are too tight.

393. What do you call a very well-dressed weed?

A dandy lion.

394. Why are rivers lazy?

Because they seldom leave their beds.

395. What are the largest ants in the world?
Gi-ants and eleph-ants.

396. What do you call a lot of girls waiting in line to buy some dolls with yellow-blonde hair?
A Barbie-queue.

397. How do baby chickens dance?
Chick-to-chick.

398. Which river in England runs between two seas?
The River Thames – because it flows between Chelsea and Battersea.

399. Where do underwater creatures go when their teeth hurt?
To a dental sturgeon.

400. What do pigs wear around their necks?
Pigs' ties.

401. What looks after small children and makes music when plucked?
A baby sitar.

402. What is small, round, smells and giggles?
A tickled onion.

403. What is very big and says, 'Fum, Fo, Fi, Fee?'
A backward giant.

404. How did the otters manage to travel at fifty miles per hour on the motorway?
By travelling in an otter-mobile.

405. What is the difference between a coyote and a flea?
One howls on the prairie, while the other prowls on the hairy.

406. What do you get if you cross a pig with an evergreen tree that has cones?
A porker-pine.

407. Why was the young glow worm a bit sad?
Because it had glowing pains.

408. Who was old, had a lot of children, and was rather sticky?
The Old Woman Who Lived In The Glue.

409. What tuba cannot be played?
A tuba toothpaste.

410. What did the male octopus say when he saw the very attractive female octopus?
'I've always got a sucker for a pretty face.'

R

RAINY DAY
411. Years ago, Mr. Smith gave his wife a large strong box and encouraged her to put something away for a rainy day. When she died, Mr. Smith opened the box – and

found seven umbrellas, six pairs of wellington boots and fourteen raincoats.

RELATIVES
412. The quickest way to find long-lost relatives is to win a fortune on the football pools.

RELIGIOUS
413. Just outside the church, the small boy found a one pound coin and picked it up.

The vicar saw the boy and said: 'Hello! I see you've found a coin. Are you going to keep it?'

'No, sir,' replied the boy

'Excellent, excellent!' beamed the vicar.

'I'm going to spend it,' said the boy.

414. Adam and Eve lived in Paradise. We know it was Paradise because Adam didn't have a mother-in-law.

415. Monica had decided to become a nun and remain a nun for the rest of her life. But after two years in the nunnery she kept having romantic thoughts about the handsome young gardener.

Eventually, one thing led to another, and immediately after the incident in the potting shed, Monica felt she had to go to the Mother Superior to confess her sin.

'I will sack the gardener immediately,' said the Mother Superior. 'And you can go and drink half a pint of vinegar while I ponder your future.'

'Vinegar!' exclaimed Monica. 'Why vinegar?'

'Because,' said the Mother Superior, 'it seems necessary to get rid of that glowing smile that's still on your face.'

416. The vicar asked the young man: 'Are you ever troubled by erotic thoughts about the opposite sex?'

'No,' replied the young man, 'I rather like the thoughts. They're no trouble.'

417. If Moses had been a lawyer, there wouldn't have been Ten Commandments. Instead there would have been many thousands of commandments, each with numerous clauses and sub-clauses.

418. Two drunks, Fred and Bill, were walking along the road when Fred said: 'Hey! Ishn't that man over th-there the Archbishop of Canterbury?'

'No,' replied Bill. 'It can't be.'

'It ish!' said Fred. 'I'll go over and ask him.'

Fred staggered over to the man and said: 'Ex . . . excuse me. But are you the . . . the Archbishop of Canterbury?'

'Get lost, you pathetic drunken creep,' replied the man, 'or I'll smash your face in!'

Fred staggered back to Bill.

'Was it the Archbish?' asked Bill.

'I don't know,' replied Fred. 'The st . . . stupid man refushed to answer my question.'

419. Jewish men are very optimistic. The proof of this is that they all have a bit cut off before they know how long it's going to be.

RESTAURANT

420. 'Waiter!' said an angry customer. 'This braised beef is disgusting. It's tough, badly cooked – generally awful. I'd like to get the chef and stuff this beef down his throat.'

'Yes, sir,' replied the waiter. 'But there are other customers ahead of you, sir, with two grilled Dover sole, a well-done steak, veal cutlets . . .'

421. Man: 'Can I have a table for dinner?'

Waiter: 'Certainly, sir. Do you want the table fried, boiled, steamed or roasted?'

422. I was once invited by a business colleague for a meal in an expensive restaurant while on a sales trip to Germany.

The whole restaurant was decorated with the stuffed heads of animals. We had to sit next to a wall on which was hung the huge head of a rhinoceros.

'My goodness!' I said to the waiter. 'That rhino looks fierce.'

'It was,' admitted the waiter. 'It killed my father.'

'I'm sorry to hear that,' I said. 'Did it happen on safari in Africa?'

'No,' said the waiter. 'It happened here in Germany. My father was sitting in a chair underneath the rhino head when it dropped off the wall and hit him.'

423. My hotel is quite nice. At dinner in the restaurant last night there was a young girl at a table next to mine. She had chicken breasts and frog's legs – but her face was beautiful.

424. Times were hard. Keith was sacked from his office job and went to work as a waiter in a restaurant. Soon after, one of his fellow redundant office workers came in.

'Fancy seeing *you* working in a place like *this*,' scoffed the man.

'So?' replied Keith. 'Fancy *you* being reduced to having to eat in a dump like this!'

425. David: 'I know this lovely little restaurant where we can eat dirt cheap.'

Barbara: 'Cheap or not, I don't fancy eating dirt.'

426. When the waiter asked my boyfriend if he wanted a fingerbowl he replied: 'No thank you, I don't eat fingers.'

ROMANCE

427. 'I saw you! I saw what you got up to last night!' said little Emily when her big sister's boyfriend came to visit.

'Oh!' said the boy, blushing. 'If you don't tell your parents I'll give you a pound.'

'That's all right,' said Emily, 'I'll only charge you fifty pence – the same as I charged the others.'

428. When I told my cousin that I'd fixed him up with a date with an attractive librarian he said: 'What part of Libraria does she come from?'

429. Catherine snuggled up to her boyfriend, Robert, and whispered: 'Darling, now that you want us to get engaged, will you give me a ring?'

Robert smiled lovingly at Catherine and replied: 'Certainly! What's your 'phone number?'

430. A friend of mine recently introduced me to his new girlfriend and said he was madly in love with her and was going to marry her in a few days' time.

I recognized her as the notorious woman who had slept with half the men in Basingstoke. I managed to get my friend into a quiet corner and broke this news to him. But he just shrugged his shoulders and said: 'So? Basingstoke's not very big.'

431. I recently overheard two women talking on a train. One said to the other: 'I hear you've broken up with John. But only last week you told me it was love at first sight.'

'I know,' came the reply, 'it *was* love at first sight. But when I saw him for the second time I went off him.'

432. I once knew a man who was very shy with women. He was much too meek to approach them, and wondered what he could do to get women to approach him instead. Then he had a bright idea and changed his name to Right as he had read that millions of women were searching for, and wanted to meet, Mr. Right.

433. My friend, Freda, has been writing to a male penfriend for eighteen months. He lives two hundred miles away.

Gradually their letters grew more and more romantic, until eventually they felt they had to meet each other.

'Unfortunately,' wrote the man, 'I am seven feet tall, have an enormous nose, and my ears stick out.'

'Don't worrry,' wrote back Freda. 'Your letters showed me your true self. But when you arrive at Paddington Station please hold a carnation in your left hand so that I can recognize you.'

434. In romance, opposites frequently attract. That is why poor young girls are often attracted to rich old men.

435. My first job was as a clerical officer and I really fancied a young typist. Eventually I plucked up enough courage and asked her: 'Could I have a date?'

'Certainly,' she replied. 'How about 1066?'

436. 'It's not fair! I've proposed to two boyfriends without avail.'

'Maybe next time you should wear a veil?'

437. My first kiss was rather romantic. I was eleven at the time and had braces to help straighten my teeth. My girlfriend wore braces on her teeth, too – and it took the fire brigade half an hour to unhook us.

438. 'Where have I seen your beautiful face before?'

'I don't know – it's always been between my ears.'

439. Somehow, I don't think I'm going to marry my current boyfriend. Last night when I casually asked him how much money he had in the bank he said he would have to go home and open the pig to find out.

440. The young girl was snuggling up to the young man on the sofa and said: 'Would you like to see my birthmark?'

'Yes,' replied the young man. 'How long have you had it?'

441. Sally and Sarah were talking about the wonderful party they had just attended.

'That George was really hunky,' said Sally.

'I know,' sighed Sarah.

'He and I got on really well,' said Sally. 'He wants to see me again and asked for my 'phone number.'

'Did you give it to him?' asked Sarah.

'I told him my number was in the 'phone book.'

'Does he know your name?'' asked Sarah.

'I told him that was in the 'phone book, too. I can't wait until he 'phones . . .'

442. Some young women are music lovers – and others can do it without.

443. Last night my girlfriend and I had a disagreement about drink. I fancied whisky and sofa, but she preferred gin and platonic.

S

SAILING

444. Suddenly, out at sea in our small sailing boat, we heard a loud noise: 'Croak, croak' it went. 'Croak, croak.' It was a frog-horn.

SALES PEOPLE

445. One door-to-door salesman does very well by using the opening line: 'Can I interest you in something your neighbour said you couldn't possibly afford?'

446. 'Humpkins!' boomed the boss. 'When I told you to fire the salesmen with enthusiasm, I did *not* want you to sack them all enthusiastically!'

447. The only orders the new trainee door-to-door salesman got were 'go away' and 'get out.'

SCHOOL

448. Teacher: 'When I was your age I could name all the Presidents of America in the right order.'

Jason: 'Sir, was that because when you were my age there had only been two or three Presidents?'

449. 'Dad, I only got one question wrong in the maths exam at school today,' said the small boy.

'That's good,' replied the father. 'How many questions were there?'

'Thirty.'

'You did very well to get twenty-nine right.'

'Not really,' said the son, 'I couldn't answer twenty-nine of them at all.'

450. I used to have a teacher at school who kept going on and on insisting that five kilos of feathers weighed the same as five kilos of lead. So one day I emptied a five kilo bag of feathers over his head and then dropped a five kilo bag of lead on him. He was rather quiet after that.

451. A friend of mine has a fifteen-year-old son at school in London. She's very worried about his progress. Although his teacher gave him an 'A' in multi-cultural assimilation, an 'A' in psycho-social awareness and another 'A' in organizational behaviourism – my friend wonders when her son is going to learn how to read and write.

452. When I went knocking on doors asking for donations

for a new school swimming pool, one peculiar person gave me a bucket of water.

453. 'Susan!' said the teacher. 'Why did you just let out that awful yell?'

'Please miss,' said Susan, 'I've just hit my fumb wiv a 'ammer.'

'Susan,' responded the teacher, 'the word is "thumb", not "fumb".'

'Yes miss,' said Susan, 'but as well as 'itting my thumb I also 'it my thinger.'

454. Where do young fish go to be educated?
Plaice school.

455. Teacher: 'How many sheep does it take to make a man's jersey?'
Small boy: 'I don't know. I didn't know sheep could knit.'

456. The biology teacher in school asked: 'What is a blood count?'
James promptly replied: 'Is it Count Dracula?'

457. When I was a boy at school and studying biology the teacher suddenly picked on me and said: 'Boy! Why is mother's milk better than other milk.'
I was so flustered that all I could think of to say was: 'mother's milk comes in more attractive containers.'

458. What tickets did the babies sell at the school summer fête?
Rattle tickets.

459. Teacher: 'If you stood facing due south, your back was north, what would be on your right hand?'
Schoolgirl: 'Fingers.'

460. Teacher: 'Samantha, where did you learn to swim so well?'
Samantha: 'In the water.'

461. What happens to plants left in the maths teacher's room?
They grow square roots.

462. The small boy in the school in Hong Kong was surprised when his teacher suddenly loomed over him and demanded: 'Are you chewing gum?'
'No,' replied the small boy, 'I'm Chiu N. Fung.'

463. Teacher: 'Simon, did your parents help you with this homework?'
Simon: 'No, miss – I got it wrong all by myself this time.'

464. Teacher: 'Now, James, can you tell me the name of a bird that cannot fly?'
James: 'A roast chicken, sir.'

465. Teacher: 'Now, Sarah, can you tell me what a skeleton is?'
Sarah: 'Yes, sir! A skeleton is a set of bones with the person scraped off.'

SCIENTISTS
466. A scientist in Oxford has spent years trying to cross a

pheasant with a guitar – he wants the pheasants to make music when they are plucked.

467. If rocket scientists are all so clever, why can they only count backwards, 10, 9, 8, 7 . . . ?

SELF EMPLOYED
468. Now I work for myself I find the greatest difficulty is when I 'phone to say I'm sick I don't know whether or not to believe myself.

SEX
469. A couple I know were having trouble with their love life so they went to seek professional help.

They were advised to put more variety into their sex lives – so now he tries to juggle and she does magic tricks while they make love.

470. A friend of mine was in New York and was approached by a prostitute.

'Would you like a good time?" asked the woman.

'How much?' asked my friend.

'What do you think I'm worth?' asked the prostitute.

'Fifty dollars?' suggested my friend.

'Cheapskate!' snapped the prostitute. 'You only get ugly trash for that sort of money!'

Later that evening my friend was with his wife waiting for a taxi outside the hotel. The prostitute happened to walk by and, as she did so, she hissed: 'See! I told you fifty dollars would only get you ugly trash!'

471. I was in a chemist's shop this morning and a very

nervous young man came in and asked for a packet of anti-sickness pills and a packet of contraceptives.

The shop assistant looked at the trembling young man, smiled, and said: 'If it makes you sick, why do it?'

472. The only reason Keith's wife says he is good in bed is because she is very houseproud and when he makes love he doesn't disturb the sheets and blankets.

473. Alison wanted to make sure that her first experience of sleeping with her boyfriend was a success, so she asked her best friend for advice.

'Why not go to a fish restaurant,' said the friend, 'and get your boyfriend to have some oysters. They are supposed to increase the sexual appetite. About half a dozen oysters should be enough.'

The next day the friend asked Alison: 'How did it go?'

'Well,' replied Alison, blushing, 'only three of the oysters seem to have worked.'

474. When Sally came home from the office unexpectedly early one day she found her handsome young husband in bed with a sixty-five-year-old woman. Sally was horrified.

Sally's husband looked up at her and said: 'Darling, this is the lady who provided your Porsche, and that nice diamond ring I gave you last week, and . . .'

'Oh,' said Sally. 'Sorry I interrupted. And can I have a necklace to match my ring?'

475. Mrs. Green was outraged. She had caught the nubile young cook kissing and cuddling in the kitchen with Mr. Green.

'If it happens again,' said Mrs. Green, 'I'll have to get another cook.'

'Oh,' replied the cook, 'I wish you would. Your husband's always said he'd fancied it with two of us.'

476. My marriage to Charles was a mistake. When he was just a boyfriend I thought he said he was over-sexed. Now I'm married to him, I realize I must have misheard him say he was over sex.

477. Albert was disappointed with his wife. Almost every night she had a headache, or was too tired, or made some other excuse not to make love.

In desperation, knowing how much his wife loved money, he told her: 'I'll put a ten pound note in the top drawer of your dressing table every time we make love.'

Soon, Albert was happy and his wife delighted in taking the ten pound notes from him for her passionate work.

Then one day Albert happened to open the top drawer of the dressing room table and saw a bundle of ten pound notes and another bundle of £20 notes – plus a number of £50 notes.

'Where did all this money come from?'' asked Albert. 'I only give you ten pound notes.'

'Well, dear,' said his wife, 'not everyone is as mean as you.'

478. Mr. Smith was always so busy working that he never had much time to spend with his son.

Then, on his son's seventeenth birthday, Mr. Smith managed to get away from his office to take his son for a birthday lunch at an expensive restaurant.

'Cor!' said the son when one of the waitresses took their coats. 'Look at the size of her boobs. I wonder what she's like in bed?'

Mr. Smith was rather alarmed at his son's comments,

but they were soon seated in the restaurant and father and son exchanged gossip and news.

Just as they were about to leave the restaurant, an attractive young woman entered.

'Wow!' exclaimed Mr. Smith's son in a loud voice. 'Her boobs are fantastic. I really fancy her.'

Mr. Smith was embarrassed. His son appeared to have turned into an uncouth, chauvinistic yob. Maybe the boy's school was to blame.

Thus it was that Mr. Smith's son was removed from the local school and sent away to the upper form in one of Britain's most expensive public schools. It was surely not too late for the boy to learn some manners.

On his son's eighteenth birthday Mr. Smith took his son to the same restaurant as before – and Mr. Smith was delighted at the way his son behaved. He was polite, well-mannered, and did not make uncouth remarks about the waitresses but treated them with charm and was a perfect gentleman.

The son talked of his plans for university, and Mr. Smith was just about to comment on the amazing transformation of his son into a man with excellent behaviour – surely the work of the public school – when the son looked at one of the waiters and said: 'Look at that! Isn't that a cute bottom? I wonder what he's like in bed.'

SEXTANT

479. The handsome young man was about to set off on a round-the-world yacht trip when his sextant was stolen.

He went into a shop on the quay and asked the new, attractive young female assistant: 'Do you have a sextant?'

'Why do it in a tent?' she asked. 'You can come back to my flat if you like.'

SHAKESPEARE
480. What would Shakespeare be doing if he was alive today?

Shouting and scratching at the lid on his coffin.

SHOOTING
481. I told my wife that we had been invited on a shooting weekend in Scotland.

'Oh good!' she said. 'Now I can see those strange birds that wear trousers.'

'Strange birds that wear trousers?' I asked.

'Yes,' she replied. 'People are always saying they shoot pheasants in braces.'

482. Last weekend I was invited on a duck shoot. Everyone shot and I had to duck.

SHOPS
483. People in Britain are becoming much stronger. Twenty years ago it would take two men to carry £10 of supermarket shopping. Now, even a small child can carry it.

484. I went to the perfume counter in a department store and asked to see and smell some different types of perfume. The assistant asked me: 'Is the perfume for your wife, sir – or would you like to see something more expensive?'

485. Business in some London shops is now so slow that when I picked up a bracelet in a jewellery shop and asked the young lady manager: 'Would you take anything off for cash?' she replied: 'For fifty pounds you can see me topless. For one hundred pounds I'll take everything off.'

486. Customer: 'I want a pen that writes underwater.'

Shop assistant: 'Wouldn't you like it to write other words, too?'

487. Customer: 'Can I have a crocodile handbag, please?'

Shop assistant; 'I'm sorry, madam, but we don't sell handbags for crocodiles.'

488. A woman went into a hardware shop and asked the assistant if he had long nails.

'Certainly!' he replied. 'But don't ask me to scratch your back with them. I've heard that tired old joke too many times.'

'I wasn't going to tell a joke,' said the woman. 'Of course I want to buy real nails, not fingernails. Can I buy some?'

'Certainly, madam,' replied the assistant. 'How long do you want them?'

The woman sighed and replied: 'At least a few years. They're to repair the kids' rabbit hutch.'

489. Yesterday I went shopping with my girlfriend and she went into the chemist's shop and asked if they had any mirrors.

'Do you want a hand mirror?' asked the sales assistant.

'No,' replied my girlfriend, 'I don't want to look at my hands in it, I want one I can see my face in.'

SISTERS

490. I wouldn't say my sister is stupid, but the other day she went into a pet shop and bought some bird seed. She thinks that if she plants it she'll grow a bird.

491. I wouldn't say my sister is desperate for a boyfriend, but when she went to the station and asked for a ticket from Bournemouth to London, the young male ticket clerk asked: 'Single?' – and she replied: 'Yes. Are you asking me for a date?'

492. My sister was asked if she'd like to be a baby sitter – but she said she thought it cruel to sit on babies.

493. My sister has visited another planet. This morning she trod on a chocolate bar and said she'd just set foot on Mars.

494. My sister isn't really fat – but when her boyfriend filled her shoe with champagne it took five bottles to do it.

495. I wouldn't say my sister was an ugly baby – but it was almost a year before my mother realized she had been putting the nappy on the wrong end.

SLEEP

496. When I asked a friend of mine if he ever woke up grumpy in the morning he said that he didn't have to – his wife had her own alarm clock.

497. When my brother was a small boy he once slept with his head under the pillow. When he woke up he found twenty-eight one-pound coins – and all his teeth were missing: the fairies had taken them.

498. Whenever I go to stay with people they always ask me how I slept. How do you think I slept? Do they think I'm odd or something? I sleep like everyone else – with my eyes closed.

499. The insomniac sheep could only get to sleep by counting people.

500. I'm very sleepy. I had to get up at the crack of yawn.

501. Last night I slept like a baby – I kept waking up and crying.

502. Last night I dreamt I was eating my pillow, so when I woke up I felt a bit down in the mouth.

SMOKING
503. I'm quite pleased with myself. I now only smoke three packets of cigarettes a day. I gave up cigarettes completely – I just smoke the packets.

504. My cousin is a chain smoker. She gave up cigarettes – now she only attempts to smoke chains.

SPEECH
505. A guarantee of freedom of speech is not much use unless there is another guarantee of freedom *after* the speech.

SPIES
506. 1st spy: 'I think Claude has become a mole.'
 2nd spy: 'How do you know?'
 1st spy: 'Because he's started eating worms and burying himself in the garden.'

SUNBURN
507. You only get really terrible sunburn if you bask for it.

SUPERSTITIOUS
508. I'm definitely *not* superstitious. It's bad luck to be superstitious.

T

TELEVISION
509. I refused to watch the new TV series about the life and times of Ethelred the Unready. It should not have been screened – there's much too much Saxon violence.

510. People say that with all the developments in television – cable, satellite, high definition TV – that TV will eventually completely replace newspapers. But have you ever tried to swat a fly with a television set?

THEATRE

511. The last time I was in London I went to a theatre ticket office and the man in front of me in the queue asked the box office clerk: 'Can I have a ticket for tonight's performance?'

'Certainly sir,' replied the clerk. 'Would you like to be in the stalls?'

'No,' said the man. 'I'm not an animal – I want a proper seat.'

512. I've just got a speaking part in the theatre. I have to walk up and down saying: 'Programmes. Would anyone like a programme?'

513. I've just been to see a hit play – most of the cast were hit by rotten eggs and tomatoes.

TIDINESS

514. Mr. Smith was fed up with his wife's insistence on absolute tidiness. He was not allowed to smoke cigarettes or cigars or a pipe at home. He had to take off his shoes before he entered the house.

His wife even made him comb his hair in the garden in case a spot of dandruff fell on the floor.

When he died, Mr. Smith managed to get some revenge. His will stipulated that his ashes were to be scattered on the lounge carpet.

TOADSTOOLS

515. How do you stop toadstools appearing in your garden?

Give the toads some sofas instead.

TRADE UNION
516. One trade union is now demanding that unskilled men get paid more than skilled men because the work is harder if people are not skilled to do it.

TRAIN TRAVEL
517. 'Why did you become a driver for British Rail?'
'It was the only way I was sure of getting a seat on a train.'

518. The only reason British Rail print timetables is so passengers know how late their trains have been.

519. I once sat next to a man on a train who had a small piece of rock in one ear. He was stone deaf.

520. Overheard conversation on a train journey:
'Clarissa is a thief, a liar and a murderer.'
'Oh – she must have improved since we were at school together.'

V

VET
521. When the budgie got sick, my children insisted I

took it to the vet for tweetment.

VITAMINS
522. The difference between a vitamin and a hormone is that you cannot hear a vitamin.

523. When I was a small boy my mother used to give me vitamins B1, B2, B6, B12 and B quiet.

W

WALK
524. Once I was out on a country walk in an area I'd never been to before. I enjoyed the beautiful scenery and soon I came to a stream – the other side of which was a country bakery from which came the delicious smell of fresh bread.

The stream was a bit too wide for me to jump across safely, but the water did not look too deep, although it was a bit muddy and I could not see the bottom.

A young girl was sitting by the side of the stream.

'Hello!' I said. 'Do you live near here?'

'Yes,' replied the girl.

'That's good,' I said. 'Then you can tell me how deep the stream is. Would I be able to walk across?'

'I think so,' replied the girl. 'The water isn't very deep.'

'Thanks,' I said, and stepped into the stream, only to sink into the water up to my neck.

'Hey!' I shouted to the girl, who was now giggling. 'I thought you said the water wasn't very deep.'

'I didn't know,' giggled the girl. 'I thought it was shallow. The water only manages to cover the legs of ducks and swans.'

WASP
525. My young son came rushing into my study shouting: 'I've been stung! I've been stung by a wasp!'

'Don't worry,' I soothed. 'I'll put some special cream on it.'

'That's no good,' said my son, 'the wasp has flown away and you'll never find it.'

WEDDING
526. I was a bit concerned on our wedding day when my husband stumbled over the words of his wedding vows, dropped the ring, and then whispered to the best man: 'Sorry! I'll do better next time.'

527. What is the point of being best man if you never get a chance to prove it?

528. A young lady I know in Hollywood has just arranged her wedding for seven o'clock in the morning – that way, if the marriage doesn't work out, she will still have most of the morning left.

WINTER
529. Winter is the time when it is too cold to do all the

boring things that it was too hot or too wet to do in Summer.

530. I always know when Winter has arrived because that is when my neighbour returns my lawnmower.

WITCH

531. What do you call an ugly old woman who sits on the beach casting spells?
  A sand witch.

532. What did the witch do when her broom broke down?
  She witch-hiked.

533. How can you easily make a witch itch?
  Remove the 'w'.

534. What do you call a witch's husband when he's travelling on her broomstick?
  A flying sorcerer.

535. What do young witches like best in school?
  Spelling lessons.

536. What do you get if a witch gets flu?
  Cold spells.

WIVES

537. I used to miss my wife every time she went away for a week to visit her mother. But now I just get in a neighbour to nag me instead.

538. When my friend Albert discovered his wife was having an affair he asked her: 'Why do you need a lover? Have you had enough of me?'

'Darling,' replied his wife, 'it's because I *haven't* had enough of you that I need a lover.'

539. If my wife has nothing to wear, why does she need three giant wardrobes to keep it in?

540. My wife makes a good living curing people. She's so ugly she hires herself out to frighten people and cure them of hiccups.

541. Claude's wife is like the Mona Lisa – she's as flat as a canvas and should be in a museum.

542. My husband says he's going to dance on my grave when I die – so today I made a new will leaving instructions that I'm to be buried at sea.

543. My wife is a wonderful magician – she can turn anything into an argument.

544. My wife has a stomach problem – she's grown so fat she can't fasten her blouse over her stomach.

545. Last night at the dinner dance my wife gave me a terrible kick that has left a nasty bruise. All I did was whisper to her that I thought her white tights looked a bit wrinkled. Unfortunately, she wasn't wearing any tights.

546. My friend John recently returned from an overseas business trip. His 'plane landed two hours early and so he rushed home to surprise his wife.

He sneaked in the back door and was just about to go upstairs when he tripped over the cat and his wife shouted from the bathroom: 'George! I thought I told you that John is expected back later today. We don't have enough time. I'll see if I can sneak next door later.'

547. The easiest way to stop a runaway horse is to get my wife to place a bet on it.

548. The much-married actor told his new girlfriend that she shouldn't believe all the tales about his bad habits – they were just old wives' tales.

549. I've had to wear pink frilly knickers ever since my wife discoverd a pair in my raincoat pocket.

550. My wife is so ugly, when we went on holiday to Africa even the mosquitoes wouldn't bite her.

551. My wife is thinking about going back to university. She's just heard that they've got a new course which she thinks is all about shopping – it's called buy-ology.

552. I think I've rather dropped myself in it. Early this morning, when I was not properly awake, my wife said: 'Darling, what would you do if I died?'

I stretched, yawned, and said: 'I don't know, dear. I love you much too much to want to think about awful things like that – especially so early in the morning.'

'But what would you do? Would you remarry?' asked my wife.

'I don't think so, dear,' I replied. 'You know I only have eyes for you. Who could possibly be as wonderful as you?'

I yawned again and then tried to go back to sleep for

another few minutes, but my wife continued her questions. 'If you did remarry,' she said, 'would your new wife wear my rings and necklaces?'

'I don't think so,' I said, without thinking, 'Aurelia's got smaller fingers and a more delicate neck than you, dear.'

553. My wife is so ugly that last night I got a 'phone call from a Peeping Tom pleading with me to get her to draw the curtains shut before she undresses for bed.

554. I wouldn't say my wife is a gossip – she just has a good sense of rumour.

555. My wife and I have somewhat different political views, but I agreed to support her when she decided to appear before the selection committee of her local Party to see if she was a suitable candidate to be the next Member of Parliament for the area in which we live.

As part of the selection process, each candidate had to give a short campaigning speech.

My wife began: 'What this country needs is much more reform. We need Electoral Reform! Social Services Reform! Education Reform! European Community Reform!'

At this point I could not hold back the words any longer and had to shout: 'And chloroform!'

556. My wife has a very clean mind – probably because she changes it every few minutes.

WORK
557. I'm not afraid of hard work – I just don't like doing any.

YUGOSLAVIA

558. My wife and I once stayed in an ancient hotel in Yugoslavia. The corridors had cobwebs and the swimming pool had green slime on it.

On the first morning of our stay we were woken by a pounding on the door.

I staggered out of bed, looked at my watch (it was 6 a.m.) and opened the door.

'Sheets!' said a plump, middle-aged maid.

'What?' I asked.

'Sheets!' repeated the maid.

'We've got sheets,' I said. 'It's only six o'clock in the morning. Surely you don't change the sheets that early? We're staying in this hotel for another three days.'

'Sheets! Give me sheets,' insisted the maid, pushing past me and into the room, whereupon she started pulling the sheets off the bed.

'This is ridiculous,' said my wife. 'Can't you leave changing the sheets until later?'

'No time,' said the maid. 'Need sheets now for breakfast.'

'Why?' I asked.

'Must have sheets,' said the maid. 'Need to put on tables as tableclothes for breakfast.'

Z

ZOO

559. Mr. and Mrs. Smith and their young daughter were on a visit to the zoo. Mr. Smith was a fitness fanatic: he went jogging for five miles every day, lifted weights, did all sorts of exercises. He was also incredibly conceited.

When they reached the cage containing the monkeys, the Smiths' daughter was entranced by the way the creatures jumped from branch to branch and did all sorts of acrobatics.

'You should see me in the gym,' said Mr. Smith. 'The stuff I do makes those monkeys look pretty boring. I do all sorts of leaps, somersaults and jumping from bar to bar and climbing ropes.'

At the cage containing the leopards, Mr. Smith boasted of his running successes and the medals he had won in various athletics events. He could, he said, even run faster than the average leopard.

By the time they reached the owls, Mrs. Smith had grown rather weary of her husband's comments. Surely Mr. Smith wouldn't feel the need to demonstrate any superiority over a humble owl. But he did.

'You know,' said Mr. Smith, 'an owl has got pretty good eyesight at night – but compared to me it's not as good. Drinking lots of carrot juice, and with lots of practice and training my eyes, I've developed excellent night vision: better than that poor owl.'

When the Smith family reached the zebra enclosure, Mrs. Smith was a bit surprised to find that two of the zebras were about to make love.

'Daddy,' said the Smiths' young daughter, 'what is that long thing between the back legs of one of the zebras?'

For once, Mr. Smith was embarrassed and he blushed as he said: 'Oh, that's nothing.'

'Huh!' said Mrs. Smith. 'There you go – boasting again!'

560. The zoo had fallen on hard times. The numbers of visitors to the zoo had fallen dramatically over the years and now the zoo was facing bankruptcy. It would have to close.

The zoo owners decided to sell all the animals and birds in the zoo at auction in an attempt to raise as much money as possible towards the zoo's debts.

Bidding was particularly good for one of the parrots. The auctioneer started the bidding at £100 and the price rapidly rose to £1,000 and the parrot was eventually sold to a young man for £1,250.

As the successful bidder wrote out a cheque, he said to the auctioneer's assistant: 'I think I got carried away with the excitement of it all. I didn't intend to pay all that much for the parrot, but as the price went up and up it seemed the bird must be really good. I hope that for £1,250 the parrot can talk a lot.'

'He certainly can,' said the auctioneer's assistant. 'Who do you think was bidding against you?'

561. Some of the animals in the zoo disliked being looked at by hordes of noisy visitors every day. They knew there was nothing they could do about their situation, but to pass away the time in their rather cramped cages and enclosures they would sometimes wonder what it would be like if they could take some revenge on their human tormentors.

'I'd like to eat that fat actor who is always bringing his

stupid children to drop coins on my head in a feeble attempt to see if I'm awake or asleep,' said one of the crocodiles.

'I agree,' replied another crocodile, 'although as I'm Jewish I wouldn't be able to eat such ham. But there are other equally dreadful people whom I could cheerfully chomp.'

'So could I,' agreed a lion. 'But the tastiest meat would probably be that well-known politician. I'd love to give him one big bite to let all the wind out of him – then what was left would be delicious: soft, fleshy and absolutely no backbone.'

WEDDING SPEECHES

This book consists *entirely* of sample wedding speeches. Every one is different, amusing, to the point, and lively. Any of them can easily be adapted to particular circumstances or delivered as it stands – with just a name changed here or there to protect the innocent!

It contains 15 speeches for the bridegroom, 15 for the best man, 12 for the bride's father, 8 for other people speaking on behalf of the bride's father, and 15 for other relations and friends who may want to say something.

SAMPLE SOCIAL SPEECHES

Sample speeches for every social occasion, including weddings. Also contains information on how to prepare and deliver a speech, as well as lots of anecdotes, aphorisms and stories for you to include in your speech.

THE RIGHT WAY TO SPEAK IN PUBLIC

Everything you need to know on how to construct a powerful speech, including how to conquer nervousness.

All uniform with this book
ELLIOT RIGHT WAY BOOKS
KINGSWOOD, SURREY, U.K.

OUR PUBLISHING POLICY

HOW WE CHOOSE

Our policy is to consider every deserving manuscript and we can give special editorial help where an author is an authority on his subject but an inexperienced writer. We are rigorously selective in the choice of books we publish. We set the highest standards of editorial quality and accuracy. This means that a *Paperfront* is easy to understand and delightful to read. Where illustrations are necessary to convey points of detail, these are drawn up by a subject specialist artist from our panel.

HOW WE KEEP PRICES LOW

We aim for the big seller. This enables us to order enormous print runs and achieve the lowest price for you. Unfortunately, this means that you will not find in the *Paperfront* list any titles on obscure subjects of minority interest only. These could not be printed in large enough quantities to be sold for the low price at which we offer this series.

We sell almost all our *Paperfronts* at the same unit price. This saves a lot of fiddling about in our clerical departments and helps us to give you world-beating value. Under this system, the longer titles are offered at a price which we believe to be unmatched by any publisher in the world.

OUR DISTRIBUTION SYSTEM

Because of the competitive price, and the rapid turnover, *Paperfronts* are possibly the most profitable line a bookseller can handle. They are stocked by the best bookshops all over the world. It may be that your bookseller has run out of stock of a particular title. If so, he can order more from us at any time—we have a fine reputation for "same day" despatch, and we supply any order, however small (even a single copy), to any bookseller who has an account with us. We prefer you to buy from your bookseller, as this reminds him of the strong underlying public demand for *Paperfronts*. Members of the public who live in remote places, or who are housebound, or whose local bookseller is unco-operative, can order direct from us by post.

FREE

If you would like an up-to-date list of all *Paperfront* titles currently available, send a stamped self-addressed envelope to
ELLIOT RIGHT WAY BOOKS, BRIGHTON RD.,
LOWER KINGSWOOD, SURREY, U.K.